CREATIVE BAKING

Deco Marshmallows

Tan Phay Shing

mc Marshall Cavendish
Cuisine

Editor: Lydia Leong
Designer: Benson Tan
All photos by Hongde Photography except step-by-step photos by Tan Phay Shing

Copyright © 2023 Marshall Cavendish International (Asia) Private Limited

Published by Marshall Cavendish Cuisine
An imprint of Marshall Cavendish International

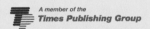

A member of the
Times Publishing Group

Other Marshall Cavendish Offices:
Marshall Cavendish Corporation, 800 Westchester Ave, Suite N-641, Rye Brook, NY 10573, USA
• Marshall Cavendish International (Thailand) Co Ltd, 253 Asoke, 16th Floor, Sukhumvit 21 Road,
Klongtoey Nua, Wattana, Bangkok 10110, Thailand • Marshall Cavendish (Malaysia) Sdn Bhd,
Times Subang, Lot 46, Subang Hi-Tech Industrial Park, Batu Tiga, 40000 Shah Alam,
Selangor Darul Ehsan, Malaysia

Marshall Cavendish is a registered trademark of Times Publishing Limited

National Library Board, Singapore Cataloguing-in-Publication Data

Name(s): Tan, Phay Shing.
Title: Deco marshmallows / Tan Phay Shing.
Other Title(s): Creative baking.
Description: Singapore : Marshall Cavendish Cuisine, [2023]
Identifier(s): ISBN 978-981-5084-19-1 (paperback)
Subject(s): LCSH: Marshmallow. | Cooking (Marshmallow)
Classification: DDC 641.853—dc23

Printed in Singapore

Dedication

To my husband Jianlong,

our children, Mun Yew and Mun Zhong,

and my mum and dad

Contents

Acknowledgements

First and foremost, I would like to thank God for providing me with the inspiration and energy to discover and create these new confections while juggling multiple responsibilities of taking care of my family and being a chef instructor.

I am immensely thankful for the support my husband gives me, whether as my visual and audio consultant for content creation, guinea pig for taste testing anything sugar-free, or sourcing for unique ingredients that I need.

I am thankful that my children are excellent at telling me what looks cute or not, and are happy to taste test my marshmallow creations and other bakes.

I am also grateful to my parents for their support and practical help, such as looking after my children whenever I need to take a break.

I would also like to thank:

Gloria and Amy for helping me to get started on my marshmallow journey, and for being so inspirational with their creativity.

Pristy for sharing her knowledge on using gel colouring for painting fine features on marshmallows.

Marshmallow Making Madness for the wealth of information on artisanal marshmallows and being a positive platform for learning and sharing about marshmallows.

Momo the plush toy bear who wants to become famous. It is my source of inspiration for the bear marshmallow entry.

Lydia, my editor, for giving me the opportunity to write this book, for her endless patience and support, and for being so accommodating of my busy schedule. I could not have asked for a better editor.

Introduction

There was a time when marshmallows were to me, nothing more than soft, fluffy candies to be eaten straight from the bag, scattered over a mug of hot chocolate or toasted over a campfire. Even though other bakers were already making character marshmallows, I never thought to explore it because marshmallows were just one-dimensional candies to me. But all that changed when someone requested to learn character marshmallows in my baking classes, leading me to study the confection in detail. It was then that I discovered that there was so much to learn, explore and share!

Being a rookie in an established field meant that there were many experts I could consult. Before I made my first marshmallow, Gloria (@miscellaneousmao) and Amy (@cookingwithamyy) shared their character marshmallow-making experiences and provided me with helpful tips. Pristy (@by.pristy) shared her knowledge on using gel colouring for painting fine features on marshmallows. The Facebook group Marshmallow Making Madness shared their wealth of knowledge about the practical aspects of marshmallow-making. I am truly grateful to each one for being part of my marshmallow-learning journey.

So what then is new and what can contribute with this book? I'm excited to share that I discovered a new method that does not rely on freehand piping on a bed of cornstarch, which is the current established method for making character marshmallows. My method uses templates which enables the baker to produce batches of deco marshmallows that are more consistent in shape and size, and are thus more aesthetically pleasing. I also discovered a way to use sugar replacements for making deco marshmallows so those on special diets would also be able to enjoy these treats.

Besides sharing my discoveries, I also include agar-based vegetarian-friendly marshmallows, a range of fillings and flavours, as well as pairings with other pastries and confections.

Although we've included *Deco Marshmallows* as part of the Creative Baking series, marshmallows do not require baking as part of the process. So instead of wishing you "Happy baking", as usual, I wish you…

Happy marshmallow-making!

Phay Shing

Basic Tools & Equipment

1 **Digital Weighing Scale**

Ingredients such as sugar and egg whites have to be weighed with precision for marshmallows to turn out well consistently. For greater accuracy, choose a digital weighing scale with 1 g increments.

2 **Measuring Spoons**

Ingredients such as salt and bottled extracts and flavours are more accurately measured using measuring spoons.

3 **Candy Thermometer**

This is for measuring the temperature of syrup when making gelatine-based marshmallows. Infra-red thermometers (for non-contact temperature measurement) and thermometers with a long metal probe both work well.

4 **Small Saucepan**

Sugar syrups are heated in a saucepan before pouring into the egg whites. Use a saucepan not more than 14 cm in diameter to ensure the syrup level is deep enough for accurate temperature measurement and even heating. A saucepan with a spout would make it easier to control the stream of hot syrup when pouring into the egg whites. It does not matter if the saucepan is stainless steel or non-stick. If you do not have a small saucepan, double the portion of ingredients suggested in the basic marshmallow recipes.

5 **Sieves**

Large fine sieves are used for sifting cornstarch or other dusting ingredients, and removing excess cornstarch from the marshmallows after they have set. Small sieves are used for sifting small quantities of powdered ingredients such as tea powders, to ensure that there are no lumps.

6 **Electric Mixer**

An electric mixer is necessary for whipping up the Italian meringue which forms the base of decorative marshmallows. You can use either a handheld or stand mixer. Many bakers use handheld mixers but I prefer the stand mixer as I find it easier when pouring the syrup and whipping the egg whites at the same time. Use a heavy metal bowl if you are using a handheld mixer as a light-weight bowl may spin around as you beat the egg whites.

7 Mixing Bowls

Mixing bowls of different sizes are needed for different applications. Use a large stainless steel bowl for making Italian meringue-based marshmallows. Wipe the bowl with paper towels and some lemon juice or vinegar to remove any residual grease as the presence of grease may affect the foaming properties of the egg whites. Use smaller mixing bowls when there are marshmallow batters of different colours. Microwaveable bowls if you need to soften the marshmallow batter using the microwave should it harden and you are unable to pipe.

8 Spatulas

A large silicone spatula is useful for scraping down the sides of the mixing bowl. Small silicone spatulas are useful for colour mixing.

9 Small Balloon Whisks

Small metal or silicone whisks are ideal when mixing gelatine in cold liquid (for gelatine-based marshmallows) or whisking agar syrup (for agar-based marshmallows) since the volume is small.

10 Piping Bags and Oriented Polypropylene (OPP) Piping Cones

Disposable plastic piping bags and piping cones of various sizes are useful for piping marshmallow batter. When very small amounts of batter or melted chocolate are needed for creating fine details such as features, piping cones made of OPP sheets provide better control of batter flow. Simply cut a sheet of OPP into a right-angled triangle and roll it up to form a cone. Cut the tip of the cone to the desired hole size and secure the top of the cone by folding it down and taping it.

11 Piping Tips

Piping tips are useful for creating specific effects on deco marshmallows. Specialised piping tips like the open-star tip or petal tip are used to create succulents and flowers respectively. Round tips are used to create shapes where symmetry is desired, such as the head and body of a Shiba Inu (page 92).

12 Baking Trays

Shallow baking trays allow for piping work to be done without obstruction.

13 Paper Templates

Paper templates ensure consistency in the designs.

14 Baking Paper

Baking paper is used to line baking trays or flower nails. Its translucency allows for the template underneath to be seen clearly for piping. Cured marshmallows also release easily from lightly greased baking paper.

15 Acetate Sheets

To lift cured marshmallows from baking paper, slide a small acetate sheet under the marshmallow. For regular-sized marshmallows, I use a 3 x 6-cm acetate sheet. For larger marshmallows, I use a larger sheet. The exact size of the sheet is not critical as long as it allows you to work with ease. Choose a sheet that is rigid enough to hold its shape but flexible enough to bend.

16 Skewer/Scribe Tool/Fine Brush

A lightly moistened skewer or scribe tool can be used to smoothen out any peaks on piped marshmallows. This tool can also be used in place of a fine brush to paint fine features on character marshmallows. Nail art brushes are particularly good for painting very fine lines.

17 Silicone Moulds/Aluminium Foil Trays

I use silicone moulds and trays made out of foil lined with baking paper to set fillings. Silicone moulds can also be used to make marshmallows of specific shapes. Simply pipe and cure marshmallows in greased moulds.

18 Food-safe Brush

Set aside a dedicated brush for removing excess dusting from marshmallows. My preference is for a soft-bristled fan-shaped brush. The soft bristles do not leave marks should you accidentally poke the marshmallow, and the fan shape is made up of two handy sides. The broad side is good for brushing dusting off large surfaces and the narrow side is ideal for brushing dusting from crevices.

19 Flower Nail

This is useful for piping floral marshmallows, especially zephyrs.

Basic Ingredients

1

Gelatine

Gelatine is what gives marshmallows their characteristic bouncy texture. This colourless, flavourless ingredient is commonly derived from animal collagen, including fish skin, pig skin, bovine hide, and beef and porcine bones. Gelatine is available in powdered or sheet forms. Although both can be used for marshmallows, I use the powdered form in this book. Gelatine needs to be soaked in cold water or other cold liquid (10°C or colder for at least 10 minutes) before it is squeezed of excess water, melted and mixed with the Italian meringue. When blooming powdered gelatine, use 1 part powdered gelatine and 4 parts water.

Using gelatine when making marshmallows can be complex as there are many factors that will affect the firmness and setting properties. As such, there is no one-size fits all recipe. The basic recipes that are shared on pages 20 (regular sugar) and 28 (sugar-free) for gelatine-based marshmallows are only guidelines. Adjust the amount of ingredients added or tweak the method according to the factors discussed below.

Source of gelatine

Fish, bovine and porcine sources of gelatine are readily available. However, some may wish to avoid using bovine or porcine gelatine. Different sources of gelatine will also have different melting points. Bovine and porcine gelatines melt at 35°C–38°C but fish gelatine melts at 24°C–27°C. My home kitchen has a temperature of 25.5°C–31°C all year round. If I were to work with fish gelatine, it would melt in the heat. This is why I choose to use bovine gelatine when I work with marshmallows at home but use fish gelatine when I teach in air-conditioned baking studios.

Bloom strength

Bloom strength is a measure of the strength and stiffness of gelatine. Gelatine for culinary purposes is available in different bloom strengths with values ranging from 125–265. Less than 150 is considered low bloom, 150–220 medium bloom and above 220 high bloom. I use bovine gelatine with 170 bloom strength in this book. Adjust the amount of gelatine used depending on the bloom strength. For example, use less gelatine (reduce by 1/2–1 tsp or 1–2 g but not more) if the bloom strength is more than 170, assuming you work in an environment similar to mine.

Ambient temperature and humidity

Gelatine is a slow-setting gel which begins to set as long as the ambient temperature is below its melting point. It can continue to set over a 24-hour period. But the lower the ambient temperature, the faster and firmer it sets. If it sets too quickly, it will interfere with piping and it would be hard to smoothen out the ridges and peaks. If this happens, try (i) reducing the amount of gelatine by 1–2 g (but not more), (ii) working in a warmer environment, preferably more than or at least 20°C, or (iii) maintaining the marshmallow batter temperature at between 27°C and 30°C in the piping bag/mixing bowl. Storing the marshmallow batter in piping bags on a tray in the oven with the heat off and light on can help.

On the other hand, working in warm, humid environments can cause the gelatine to set more slowly. Leave the marshmallows out to cure for at least 8 hours or in the refrigerator for 30 minutes to 2 hours before coating/dusting. Working in an air-conditioned room can help the gelatine in marshmallows set faster.

Inhibitors

The presence of inhibitors to gel formation will weaken gelatine strength and prevent marshmallows from setting properly, if at all. Examples of inhibitors include:

- Strong acids such as citrus juices

- Ingredients with high alcohol concentration (above 40%)

- Ingredients with high salt concentration

- Prolonged heat exposure (above 60°C)

- Enzymes found in ginger root and fresh fruits such as kiwi, papaya, pineapple, peach, mango, guava and fig. Bringing these fresh fruits to a simmer will deactivate these enzymes.

If the inhibitor cannot be eliminated, add more gelatine (increase by ½–1 tsp or 1–2 g) to compensate for the loss in gel strength.

2

Agar

Like gelatine, agar is a common gelling agent used in food and beverages. It is derived from seaweed, making it vegetarian-friendly. (Note though that my agar-based marshmallows are not vegan as they contain egg whites.) Agar is available in different bloom strengths. The typical range is 700–1,200 with 900 being the standard strength. As agar has much higher bloom strengths than gelatine, the resulting marshmallows are firmer and have a different texture.

Agar usually comes in the form of powder or flakes. I use the powdered form with a bloom strength of 700 in this book. Agar powder needs to be dispersed in room temperature or cold liquid for 10 minutes before bringing to a boil and simmering for 3–5 minutes. It can then be mixed with the substance to set. The inhibitors to gel formation for gelatine apply to agar, except that agar is able to tolerate higher heat treatment as its melting point is between 85°C and 95°C. Adjust the amount of agar used according to bloom strength and presence of any inhibitors.

Agar sets at around 38°C and 40°C, which is why there is no need to cure or set agar-based marshmallows in the refrigerator, even in warmer environments. Agar sets much faster than gelatine, so work quickly when making agar-based marshmallows. Note though that curing agar-based marshmallows in humid environments takes a longer time, usually about 1–2 days.

3

Sugar

Castor or granulated white sugar is typically used to make regular gelatine and agar-based marshmallows but other sugars can be used too.

Brown sugar will add a caramel tone but as brown sugar, especially dark brown sugar, is more hygroscopic than white sugar, the marshmallows will be moister. Brown sugar syrups will also boil a lot higher in the saucepan so make sure to use an extra tall saucepan to prevent the syrup from boiling over.

Sugar replacements can be used to make diabetic-friendly or keto marshmallows, but the substitution is not a straightforward one. Note that some people may also have digestive sensitivities to alcohol sugars. The sugar-free marshmallows in this book are made using allulose. I do not use xylitol as it can be harmful to house pets if accidentally ingested. Although erythritol is the most commonly available and widely accepted zero calorie/zero Glycaemic Index sugar replacement, it is not ideal for marshmallow-making as it tends to recrystallise easily, causing the marshmallows to turn gritty. As a bonus, allulose also tastes less sweet than white sugar for the same amount used.

4

Egg Whites

Although marshmallows can be made without egg whites, this book covers piped decorative marshmallows using an Italian meringue base. Italian meringue is made from egg whites and it allows the marshmallow batter to remain in pipeable consistency for longer.

Always use fresh egg at room temperature to ensure the best outcome for your marshmallows. Keep the egg whites free of any traces of egg yolk and the mixing bowl grease-free to enable the meringue to whip up properly. Note that the meringue may take a longer time to whip up in humid environments.

If you have concerns about using raw egg whites in marshmallows, you may use reconstituted egg white powder or meringue powder with water. While vegan egg white substitutes such as plant protein and aquafaba are available, they will not be covered in detail in this book.

5 Inverted Sugar

Inverted sugar is a sweet syrup made up of fructose and glucose. In marshmallow-making, inverted sugar is added to retain moisture and softness, as well as to prevent crystallisation in the sugar syrup as the presence of sugar crystals can cause marshmallows to be gritty.

Examples of inverted sugar that can be used are light corn syrup, dark corn syrup, honey, maple syrup and agave syrup. I use light corn syrup as it is colourless. Omit inverted sugar when making diabetic-friendly/keto marshmallows because all forms of inverted sugar will contribute to a rise in blood sugar levels. This omission is not an issue for my sugar-free marshmallows as allulose does not recrystallise when dissolved and marshmallows made with allulose tend to retain moisture too.

6 Liquids

In marshmallow-making, liquids are needed in the gelatine/agar bloom and sugar syrup. The most common liquid used is water as it does not affect the gelling properties of gelatine and agar, and it is also colourless. Other liquids such as juice, fruit and vegetable purées, coffee, low alcohol drinks and tea infusions can also be used. They add interesting flavours and colours to the marshmallows and can even temper the sweetness levels. When using acidic or alcoholic liquids, use more gelatine (increase by ½–1 tsp or 1–2 g), to compensate for the reduction in gelling strength. Use 1 part gelatine and 3 parts cold water. You may also add acidic liquids to the syrup instead of the gelatine bloom. Thick fruit/vegetable purées are used in the meringue for agar-based marshmallows and the liquid in the sugar syrup is usually water.

7 Lemon Juice

Lemon juice is a natural source of acid added to the Italian meringue base to help to stabilise the meringue. Lemon juice can also help temper the sweetness level of marshmallows. An alternative to lemon juice is cream of tartar.

8 Extracts and Emulsions

Any commercially-available extract and emulsion can be used as long as they are not oil-based since these will cause the meringue to deflate and the marshmallows to become runny. Extracts and emulsions are added to the marshmallow batter after it is whipped up, to the sugar syrup or to the gelatine bloom. Refrain from adding more than the amount indicated in the recipes to avoid the flavour becoming overpowering.

9   Dusting/Coating

Marshmallows have sticky surfaces even after curing and can be especially sticky in humid environments. A layer of dusting or coating will help. The most common dusting is a sifted mixture of icing sugar and cornstarch. In humid climates, a cornstarch-only dusting is recommended to prevent the marshmallows from sticking to each other and the container during storage. Refer to page 37 for more ideas on preventing marshmallows from sticking.

10   Oil

This is not an ingredient added to marshmallows but it is essential in the preparation process. A thin coat of oil is applied to the baking paper placed over the template for piped marshmallows. An oil spray can also be used to grease silicone moulds for ease of releasing marshmallows set in moulds.

11   Gel Colouring

I use gel colouring as the colours are vibrant and it does not affect the consistency of the marshmallow. Note that some colours like red, green and blue may deepen with time so take this into account when using these colours. Dried gel food colouring is used for painting fine features without adding too much moisture since gel colouring straight from the bottle will cause painted features to spread or smudge during storage.

12   Charcoal Powder

I use charcoal powder instead of black gel colouring when I need to colour a small amount of marshmallow mixture black for pipping fine facial features on characters. A drop or two of warm water may be added if the consistency of the mixture becomes too thick after adding the powder.

13   Sprinkles

Sprinkles can add colour and variety when used as features or accessories on decorative marshmallows.

14   Chocolate

I use melted dark chocolate or white chocolate/coloured white chocolate to add small details where appropriate. It helps to melt the chocolate with a little oil or shortening so it remains in a pipeable consistency for a longer time before solidifying.

Basic Gelatine-Based Marshmallows

Fish, porcine or bovine gelatine may be used. In this book, I use bovine gelatine with 170 bloom strength. The marshmallows are prepared and piped in my hot (25.5°C–31°C) and humid kitchen with a relative humidity of 60%–90%. I let the marshmallows set, then dust and pack them in an air-conditioned room (21°C–24°C) with a relative humidity of 40%–60%. Your working environment and choice of gelatine may differ. Make the necessary adjustments (refer to section on gelatine, page 15). This recipe makes 25–30 marshmallows, each 4 cm in size.

Gelatine Bloom

32 g ice water

8 g gelatine powder

1 tsp vanilla extract

Italian Meringue

60 g fresh egg whites, room temperature

½ tsp lemon juice or ¼ tsp cream of tartar

10 g and 140 g castor sugar, separated

60 g light corn syrup

⅛ tsp salt

40 g water

Finishing

Gel food colouring

Cornstarch for dusting

1. Place 4-cm circle template (page 130) on baking tray, then line with baking paper. Apply a thin layer of oil on baking paper.

2. Bloom gelatine by scattering it a little at a time over ice water in a small bowl. (Use a microwave-safe bowl if using the microwave to melt gelatine.) Whisk after each addition until well combined. Pour vanilla on top of bloom. Set aside.

3. Make Italian meringue. Place egg whites, lemon juice/cream of tartar and 10 g sugar in the mixing bowl of a stand mixer. Mix using a whisk attachment at the lowest speed until sugar is dissolved.

4. In the meantime, heat 140 g sugar, corn syrup, salt and water in a small saucepan without stirring. Gently swirl saucepan as necessary. Monitor sugar temperature.

5. When syrup starts to boil, increase mixer speed to medium and whisk egg whites until soft peaks form. Test by lifting the whisk up to form a peak in the meringue. It should melt back in within a few seconds. Check if syrup has reached 114°C. If not, reduce mixer speed to minimum and continue to monitor syrup temperature.

6. Once temperature reaches 114°C–116°C (use higher temperature if your environment is hot and humid), remove from heat and increase mixer speed to medium-high. Slowly pour syrup down sides of mixing bowl. Continue beating for 2 minutes.

7. In the meantime, melt bloomed gelatine in a microwave or by using the residual heat of a saucepan. If the former, heat at medium-low power in 10-second bursts. If the latter, transfer bloomed gelatine to a hot empty saucepan and stir until gelatine is fully melted.

8. Slowly pour melted gelatine into egg white mixture. Beat for another 5 minutes or until mixture is able to hold its shape. Note that different consistencies are required for different designs (page 35).

9. Add gel food colouring. Mix well using a mixer at low speed or with a silicone spatula.

 Scan the QR code to view a video tutorial on making basic gelatine-based marshmallows.

10. Transfer mixture to a large piping bag. Cut a 1-cm hole at the tip. The actual size of the hole is not important as long as you are able to control the flow of the marshmallow mixture from the bag. Use a 1-cm wide piping tip if you prefer more consistent round shapes.

11. Dab corners of baking paper with marshmallow batter to hold it down. Pipe mounds on prepared baking tray. Position tip of piping bag about 1 cm away from tray. Apply constant pressure on piping bag while slowly moving it upwards as you squeeze. Release pressure on piping bag and give the tip a twirl to lift off.

12. Use a skewer or scribe dipped in water to smoothen any bumps or bubbles on marshmallow surface. Alternatively, use a damp finger to tap down any bumps.

13. Leave piped marshmallows to set overnight or for at least 8 hours. Do this in an air-conditioned room if your environment is warm. If in a hurry, refrigerate for 30 minutes to 2 hours. Note that marshmallows will continue to set for up to 24 hours. Marshmallows left to set for longer will have a smoother and shinier finishing after dusting.

14. Sift a light coating of cornstarch/other dusting (page 37) over set marshmallows then brush to ensure marshmallows are thoroughly coated. Use a small acetate sheet to carefully dislodge marshmallows from baking paper with a gentle to-and-fro motion, pushing dusting under base of marshmallows at the same time. Never use brute force as this may damage the base.

15. Toss marshmallows in a sieve to remove excess dusting. Do this a few at a time.

16. Store in an airtight container at cool room temperature. Consume within 2 weeks.

Basic Agar-Based Marshmallows (Zephyr)

Dating back to medieval times, zephyr or zefir is still one of the most popular treats in modern Eastern Europe. Zephyrs are agar-based marshmallows made from fruit purée, usually apples, various types of berries and other high pectin fruits. This recipe makes 20–25 marshmallows, each about 5-cm in size.

Apple Jam

100 g apple purée (*see* Note)
20 g lemon juice
$\frac{1}{4}$ tsp salt
100 g castor sugar

Meringue

Apple jam (150–160 g)
1 egg white (35–40 g)

Agar Syrup

160 g castor sugar
5 g agar powder
20 g light corn syrup
80 g water

Gel food colouring
Cornstarch/Icing sugar for dusting

Note: To make apple purée, halve 2–3 Granny Smith apples and remove core. Place cut-side down on a lined baking tray. Bake in a preheated oven at 180°C (top and bottom heat only, no fan) for 30 minutes or until soft. Leave to cool completely. Discard skin and press baked apple through a fine-mesh sieve. Store refrigerated in an airtight container if not using immediately. You may prepare this ahead of time

1. Prepare apple jam. Weigh empty saucepan before using. Add all ingredients and cook over medium-low heat, stirring often to prevent jam from burning or sticking to base of pan. Cook until contents of saucepan weigh about 170 g. Set aside to cool to room temperature. You may prepare this ahead and store refrigerated in a clean airtight container.

2. Before making marshmallows, have everything prepared as agar-based marshmallows set much faster than gelatine-based marshmallows. Prepare baking tray with 5-cm circle template (page 131) and line with baking paper. For the traditional swirl, I used tip #868 but any open-star tip would do. Fit tip into a large piping bag.

3. Place apple jam and egg white in a clean stand mixer bowl. Whisk to loosen jam and mix well with egg whites. Let jam mixture come to room temperature if ingredients are cold from fridge.

4. In a small saucepan, whisk sugar and agar powder together to disperse agar and prevent clumping. Add water and whisk briefly. Let agar sit for 10 minutes. Add light corn syrup and whisk. The sugar does not need to be dissolved.

5. Prepare meringue. Beat egg whites on medium speed until firm peaks form. Test by lifting whisk to form a peak in the meringue. The peak should stand up straight with a slight curl at the end. Lower mixer speed to minimum while preparing agar syrup.

6. Bring agar syrup to a boil over medium heat while whisking constantly. Reduce heat to medium-low and whisk for another 5 minutes. Start monitoring syrup temperature at this point. If using a candy thermometer with a probe, note that sticking the probe in too early will give an inaccurate reading as the syrup will solidify and coat the probe.

7. Once syrup reaches 105°C–110°C or when any attempt to drip syrup from the whisk forms threads instead of droplets, remove from heat.

8. Turn mixer speed to medium-high and slowly pour syrup down sides of mixing bowl. Continue beating for 3–5 minutes or until mixture starts to peel away from sides of bowl and clumps up a little on whisk, which may happen sooner than 3 minutes. The mixture should maintain stiff peaks when whisk is lifted.

9. Add gel food colouring and mix well using a spatula. Transfer to a piping bag.

10. Dab corners of baking paper with marshmallow batter to hold it down. Pipe swirls on prepared baking tray. Position tip of piping bag 1–2 cm away from tray and over centre of circle on template. Apply constant pressure while piping. Release pressure on piping bag and give tip a twirl to lift off.

11. Leave piped marshmallows to set overnight or for at least 8 hours. Do this in an air-conditioned room if your environment is warm. You may need a longer drying time (1–2 days) if the environment is humid, the jam contains more moisture from the apples or the agar syrup contains more water.

12. Sift a light coating of cornstarch or icing sugar over set marshmallows. Alternatively, dab with a brush. Zephyrs are traditionally dusted with icing sugar but this is not suitable for humid environments. Carefully peel marshmallows off the baking paper. Leave to set longer if it remains stuck. Dust marshmallows with a brush to remove any excess dusting.

13. Store in an airtight container at cool room temperature. Consume within 2 weeks. See page 42 for more storage details.

Variation

To make these vegan, replace the egg white with 40–45 g reduced aquafaba and lower the amount of salt added to ⅛ tsp.

To obtain aquafaba, shake a 425-g can of chickpeas before opening it, then drain the chickpeas and reserve the brine. Pass the brine through a sieve to remove any chickpea fragments. Place in a saucepan and cook over low heat, stirring occasionally until the brine is reduced to 40% of its original weight. Cover and refrigerate overnight before using.

 Scan the QR code to view a video tutorial on making basic agar-based marshmallows.

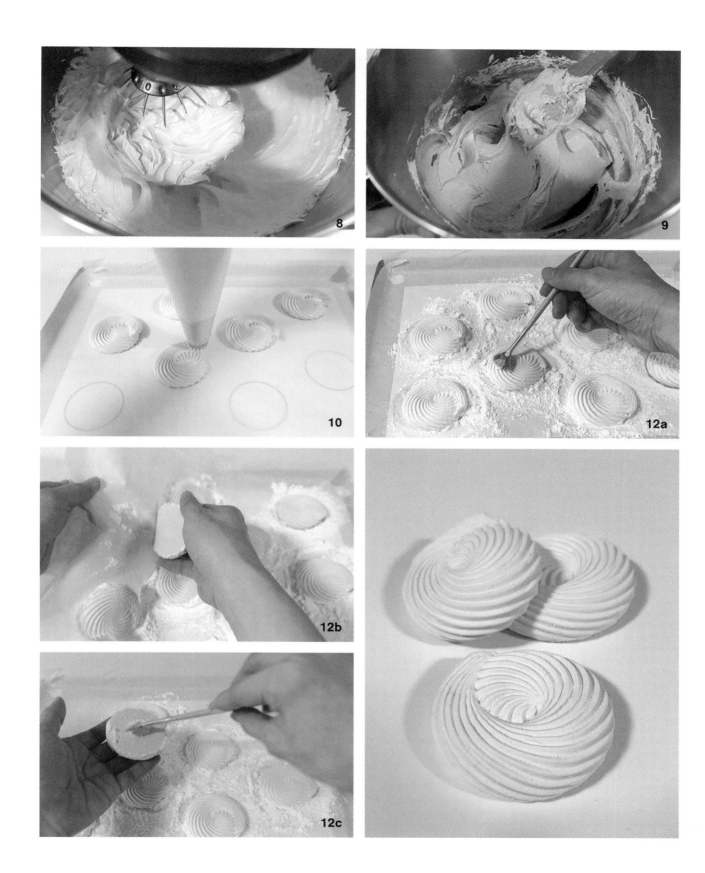

Basic Sugar-Free Marshmallows

When replacing white sugar with sugar replacements, the substitution is not a simple 1:1 ratio as sugar-replacements do not have the same candy-making properties as sugar. Allulose syrup contains higher water concentration even when brought to a high syrup temperature and tends to caramelise and burn more easily. It also tastes significantly less sweet than regular sugar when the same amount is used. Inverted sugars are omitted in making allulose-based marshmallows as it is not necessary as an addition to prevent crystallisation since allulose does not crystallise after dissolving. This is why more gelling agent and sugar-replacement is used for the same amount of egg whites as compared to using regular sugar.

Sugar-Free Gelatine-Based Marshmallows

Gelatine Bloom

48 g ice water

16 g gelatine powder (do not use fish gelatine due to its low melting point)

1 Tbsp vanilla extract (to mask the taste of allulose and gelatine)

Italian Meringue

60 g fresh egg whites at room temperature

½ tsp lemon juice or
¼ tsp cream of tartar

20 g allulose

200 g allulose

⅛ tsp salt

50 g water

Gel food colouring

Cornstarch for dusting

Modification to Steps

1. Follow recipe using regular sugar except that the sugar syrup should be brought to 118°C.

2. Store sugar-free gelatine-based marshmallows refrigerated in an airtight container lined first with paper towels, then baking paper.

Sugar-Free Agar-Based Marshmallows

Apple Jam

100 g apple purée

20 g lemon juice

¼ tsp salt

100 g allulose

Meringue

Apple jam (150–160 g)

One egg white (35–40 g)

Agar Syrup

200 g allulose

7 g agar powder

80 g water

Gel food colouring

Cornstarch or powdered erythritol
  for dusting

Note: Sugar-free agar-based marshmallows do not have a zero glycaemic index as fruits are used.

Modification to Steps

1. Follow recipe using regular sugar except that the sugar syrup should be brought to 110°C–115°C or heated until it drips in threads rather than droplets when the whisk is lifted.

2. Store sugar-free gelatine-based marshmallows refrigerated in an airtight container lined first with paper towels, then baking paper.

Flavouring Gelatine-Based Marshmallows

Commercially-Available Extracts and Emulsions

Extracts and emulsions can be added to the sugar syrup or to the top of the gelatine bloom. Note though that the extracts and emulsions should not be oil-based nor contain any substances that can affect the structure of the meringue or gelatine. Popular extracts and emulsions include vanilla, coconut, mint, caramel, pandan, ube, various types of fruits, various types of nuts, coffee, chocolate, cotton candy and cream cheese. Chocolate emulsions are particularly helpful when defatted cocoa powder is not available and you want a chocolate flavour.

Fruits

Reduced fruit juices, purées and reconstituted freeze-dried fruit powders tend to trap moisture. If using, the syrup needs to be brought to firm ball stage at 118°C–120°C.

Fruits Containing Protein-Destroying Enzymes

Examples of such fruits include mango, pineapple, kiwi, guava and papaya. Deactivate the enzymes by heating the finely sieved purées or juices. Reducing the purées/ juices through prolonged low heat (barely simmering) can also help to thicken them and intensify the flavour. I reduce juices to 40% of original weight and purées to 60% of original weight. Use chilled reduced purée/juice to bloom gelatine powder. If you would like to add more flavour, replace part or all of the water for sugar syrup with purée/juice. Stir the fruit-based sugar syrup occasionally to prevent it from burning and boiling up too high.

Sour Citrus

Sour citrus fruits include lemon, lime, grapefruit and yuzu. You may use either 100% juice concentrate from the bottle or freshly-squeezed citrus juice. Due to the high acidity of sour citrus, the amount of gelatine has to be increased — use 10 g instead of 8 g. Replace ice water with chilled citrus juice or juice concentrate.

Orange

Although orange is a citrus fruit, its level of acidity is not high and the amount of gelatine used need not be increased. Freshly-squeezed orange juice is however mild and would need to be concentrated. As boiling would compromise its flavour, orange juice has to be concentrated by freezing. To do this, fill a freezer-safe container with freshly-squeezed orange juice and freeze overnight. The next day, let it sit at room temperature for the frozen juice to melt. When the frozen juice is almost completely melted, refrigerate the container and leave it to sit undisturbed for a few days. Concentrated orange juice will settle to the bottom, leaving a layer of clear water above it. Carefully remove the top layer of clear water without disturbing the concentrated juice at the bottom. Chill the orange juice concentrate and use it to bloom gelatine and replace the water in the sugar syrup. Although orange zest can boost the orange flavour, adding it to marshmallow batter is not ideal as the specks of zest will be visible and the oil from the peel may deflate the meringue. Use a few drops of orange extract if necessary.

Fruit and Berries

Freeze-dried fruit powders offer a fuss-free way of adding intense flavour through a natural source. Flavours such as raspberry, blueberry and strawberry are available from baking supply and health food stores. Stir 12–15 g freeze-dried berry powder into 30 g hot water to form a smooth paste. Strain paste to remove any lumps, then cover and refrigerate until chilled. Use chilled paste to bloom gelatine. Alternatively, use freshly sieved berry purée and reduce to 60% of its original weight. The chilled purée can be used to bloom gelatine. It can also replace half or all of the water in the sugar syrup.

Passionfruit

Use freeze-dried passionfruit powder or sieved passionfruit pulp. If using freeze-dried powder, mix 12 g with 30 g hot water to form a paste. Follow the same instructions as freeze-dried berry powder. If using fresh passionfruit purée, there is no need to reduce it as the flavour is already intense. Use chilled passionfruit purée to bloom gelatine and replace half of the water in the syrup with passionfruit purée. Passionfruit can also be paired with honey; simply replace light corn syrup with honey as the inverted sugar.

Brown Sugar Caramel

For a light caramel note, replace white sugar with dark brown sugar. For a more intense flavour, replace light corn syrup with dark corn syrup. Caramel extract can also boost the caramel flavour. Heat syrup to 115°C–118°C as brown sugar contains more moisture than white sugar. Note that brown sugar syrup will boil up a lot higher so use a tall saucepan and whisk the syrup to keep the syrup from boiling over the rim.

Tea

Powdered Tea Matcha, hojicha and kocha are examples of tea powders that can be used. Dissolve 8-10 g tea powder in 32 g hot water. Cover and refrigerate until chilled. Use the chilled tea to bloom gelatine.

Brewed Tea Brew concentrated tea by steeping 10 g dried tea leaves or flowers in 100 g boiling hot water. Steep for 10 minutes before squeezing out teabags. Portion out 32 g and chill for blooming gelatine. Portion out 40 g for replacing water in sugar syrup.

Coffee

Add 5–7 g instant coffee granules to unwhipped egg whites. If using brewed coffee, brew a strong coffee of choice, then chill and use to bloom gelatine. It can also be used to replace water in sugar syrup.

Gingerbread

Substitute light corn syrup with dark corn syrup. Substitute half the castor sugar with dark brown sugar. Bring syrup temperature to 115°C–118°C as brown sugar contains more moisture than white sugar. Note that brown sugar syrup boils up a lot higher than regular sugar so use a tall saucepan. Add 1 Tbsp gingerbread spice mix to the syrup ingredients before boiling it. Make gingerbread spice mix by combining 2½ tsp cinnamon, 1 tsp ground ginger, ½ tsp nutmeg and ¼ tsp cloves. Dust marshmallows with gingerbread spice mixed with functional dusting of choice for a stronger boost in flavour.

Flavouring Agar-Based Marshmallows

Unlike gelatine-based marshmallows, extracts and emulsions are not usually added to agar-based marshmallows as the fruit content is high enough to impart sufficient flavour. Extracts and emulsions can however be added to complement the fruity base of the marshmallows, if desired. They can be added to the marshmallow batter after it is whipped up or to the agar syrup. Note though that the extracts and emulsions should not be oil-based nor contain any substances that can affect the structure of the meringue or gelling agent.

Below is a list of flavours from natural or whole food sources which are suitable for both regular and sugar-free options. Granny Smith apples used as the base in most zephyrs impart a mild fruity flavour that can complement many flavours.

Strawberries, Cherries and Berries

Strawberries, cherries, raspberries and blackberries are fruits used in many classic zephyr recipes because they provide fresh fruity flavours that counteract the sweetness of sugar and add natural colouring in lovely shades of pink and purple. The method of making zephyrs from these fruits is the same as the basic apple-based zephyr (page 24), with part of the apple purée replaced by fruit purée. Zephyrs still require some apple purée since strawberries, cherries and berries have high water content and are low in pectin. To prepare strawberry, cherry and berry purée, press the fresh or defrosted frozen fruit through a fine sieve. To make the jam, replace 100 g apple purée with 70 g fruit purée and 70 g apple purée, and reduce until mixture weighs 170 g.

Mango

Mango imparts a lovely tropical flavour to marshmallows. To make the jam, replace 100 g apple purée with 80 g finely sieved mango purée and 40 g apple purée, and reduce until mixture weighs 170 g.

Passionfruit

Passionfruit has a an intense flavour that offsets the sweetness of sugar, making it a wonderful flavouring for marshmallows. But as passionfruit purée is runny and has low pectin content, it needs to be mixed with apple purée, and reduced. To make the jam, replace 100 g apple purée with 70 g passionfruit purée and 70 g apple purée, and reduce until mixture weighs 170 g. Passionfruit may be paired with mango for a tangy tropical flavour.

Matcha

Matcha imparts an earthy green colour and tea flavour, and tempers the sweetness of the marshmallow. Whisk together 2–3 tsp (6–9 g) matcha powder with agar and sugar/allulose mixture in a saucepan, then add water. Using a dusting of cornstarch/icing sugar and matcha powder if desired. For a delightful combination with complex flavours, add 1–2 tsp (3–6 g) matcha powder when making raspberry or strawberry agar-based marshmallows.

Black Tea

Black tea pairs very well with apple. Brew concentrated black tea by steeping 12 g tea leaves (about 6 teabags) in 120 g boiling water. Steep for 10 minutes before squeezing out teabags. Portion out 80 g to replace water in agar syrup. If you have access to instant black tea powder, add 10 g to saucepan with ingredients for agar syrup.

Coffee

Brew a strong coffee and use 80 g to replace water in agar syrup. Alternatively, whisk 6–8 g instant coffee granules with egg whites and apple jam mixture.

Pumpkin

To prepare pumpkin purée, cut a pumpkin in half and scoop out seeds and stringy bits. Place cut-side down on a lined baking tray. Bake in an oven preheated to 180°C for 45–60 minutes or until flesh is soft. Adjust baking time according to size of pumpkin. Press baked pumpkin through a fine mesh sieve to make purée. Replace 100 g apple purée with 140 g pumpkin purée and reduce lemon juice to 5 g. Follow instructions for basic apple-based recipe on page 24. To make pumpkin spice latte zephyrs, add a dash of pumpkin spice and replace half the water in the agar syrup with brewed coffee or add instant coffee granules to egg whites.

Batter Consistency

Agar-based marshmallows only have one working consistency, which is stiff. There is thus no need to adjust the piping consistency. The need to adjust piping consistency only applies to gelatine-based marshmallows.

Regular Piped Marshmallow Consistency

As seen in the basic recipe for gelatine-based marshmallows (page 20), the consistency for piping fluffy marshmallows is what I call floppy peaks where the marshmallow batter roughly holds its piped shape but any peaks in the piped shape can be easily flattened with a damp skewer or damp finger.

Consistency can be varied within this range. For example, when piping a tall mound for a character in an upright position such as the cat (page 80), a stiffer consistency would be ideal. This can be achieved by heating the sugar syrup to 117°C–119°C. The Italian meringue is whipped for 3 minutes instead of 2 minutes, or until the meringue consistently peels off the sides of the mixing bowl (see photo) before adding melted gelatine. Beat marshmallow batter for 3–4 minutes until firm peaks form. Marshmallow batter made with this consistency is able to hold a firm peak when you raise the whisk slowly. A firm peak is a peak that stands upright with a small curl at the end.

Stiff Consistency

Gelatine-based piped marshmallows do not have a very sharp definition due to the nature of the gelling agent used. To make a stiff batter that is able to hold the ridges created by a piping tip, heat the sugar syrup to 120°C–125°C to the hard ball stage. This will also have the effect of reducing the water content. Whip the Italian meringue for 3 minutes or until the meringue consistently peels off the sides of the mixing bowl before adding the melted gelatine. Beat the marshmallow batter until melted gelatine is thoroughly incorporated and batter remains stiff. This will take 1½-3 minutes.

Runny Consistency

A runny batter consistency is ideal for piping or painting fine features or flat details. To achieve this for a small amount of batter, start from the regular consistency, then add a few drops of warm water at a time. Stir and briefly heat in the microwave oven at medium power for 3 seconds. Adjust the amount of water added according to your preferred consistency. Be careful not to add too much water or the marshmallows may not set and the colouring may run. Use the batter before it sets to a firmer consistency. Note that the batter should not be heated too many times as this will cause meringue to break down.

To make a full batch of batter with runny consistency, heat the syrup to 110°C–113°C and whip the marshmallow batter for 3–4 minutes. Batter at runny consistency is not able to hold a peak at all.

Dusting / Coating

Besides preventing marshmallows from sticking to each other or the storage container, dusting/coating can add texture, flavour and colour to your creations.

Functional Dusting

The standard functional dusting ingredient is cornstarch or an equal mixture of icing sugar and cornstarch. Tapioca starch and arrowroot powder can be used in place of cornstarch. Powdered erythritol can be used as substitute for icing sugar. Arrowroot powder and powdered erythritol are diabetic-/keto-friendly options but may not be as easily available. The ratio of the dusting ingredients can be adjusted according to taste preference and humidity. For example, use 3 parts icing sugar to 1 part cornstarch (by weight) if your environment is dry. Although cornstarch is most commonly used, some dislike the floury taste and mouthfeel. A dusting purely of icing sugar may be used if humidity permits.

Freeze-Dried Fruit Powders

Freeze-dried fruit powders such as raspberry, strawberry, blueberry, mango and passionfruit add flavour and colour to marshmallows. They can be added to the marshmallow batter and/or used as a coating. But given the hygroscopic nature of these powders, they should be mixed well with a functional dusting to prevent the absorption of excess moisture from the surroundings which could cause the marshmallows to become sticky. The standard ratio is 1 part freeze-dried fruit powder to 4 parts functional dusting of choice, but the proportions can be adjusted to accommodate taste preferences and humidity levels.

Cocoa Powder

I do not add cocoa powder to the batter for meringue-based marshmallows as such powders have a significant percentage of fat which will deflate the meringue. Instead, I use cocoa powder for dusting. Mix the cocoa powder with an equal amount of functional dusting. Cornstarch and tapioca starch work best in humid environments.

Tea Powders

Tea powders like matcha and hojicha are great for dusting. Mix 1 part tea powder with 2 parts functional dusting.

Spice Powders

Cinnamon is the most commonly used spice in marshmallow-making as it complements other flavours such as coffee, caramel and brown sugar. Mix it with cocoa powder for a chocolate spice coating, or a mixture of spices to create a gingerbread spice/pumpkin spice coating. Be careful not to use too much spice as it can be overpowering and leave a bitter taste. The standard ratio is 1 part spice powder to 12 parts functional dusting.

Sanding Sugar

Sanding sugar is coarse-grained sugar and it is available in bright colours. Instead of purchasing individual colours, make your own by mixing a drop of gel food colouring or a pinch of powdered food colouring with uncoloured sanding sugar in a resealable bag. Shake and massage the bag until the sugar is evenly coloured.

Coating marshmallows with sanding sugar will give your character marshmallows a furry, sparkly look, but note that it is not recommended for humid environments. Sanding sugar may be used directly to coat cured marshmallows without functional dusting. To create a furry look for your character marshmallows without the added sugar, use desiccated coconut. Match the colour of your character marshmallow with the sanding sugar/ desiccated coconut for an aesthetically-pleasing appearance.

Desiccated Coconut

Marshmallows coated with desiccated coconut have a "furry look" as well as a lovely toasted coconut aroma (when toasted) and a distinctive fibrous texture. Desiccated coconut can be used to coat cured marshmallows without the need to add functional dusting. If you prefer it fine and even, grind using a coffee or spice grinder and sift. As mentioned above, desiccated coconut can be coloured to match the colour of your marshmallow. To do this, use gel food colouring diluted in water. Place the desiccated coconut in a resealable bag or mixing bowl and add the colouring a little at a time until the desired shade is achieved. Spread the coloured desiccated coconut out in a thin layer on a lined baking tray or baking mat. Bake at 90°C until dry to the touch. The drying time will vary depending on how much water was added. Use immediately or store in airtight container.

Ground or Chopped Nuts

Whether ground or chopped, toasted nuts add bite, flavour and texture to marshmallows. Grind or chop, then sift to have it as fine or as coarse as desired. Take note to pulse the grinder to avoid getting nut butter. Ground or chopped toasted nuts can be used directly to coat cured marshmallows without the need to be mixed with functional dusting.

Crushed Cookies

Oreo cookies (cream scraped), Biscoff biscuits and Graham crackers can be crushed and used as a coating for cured marshmallows without the need for functional dusting. Note though that crushed cookies will turn soft as they absorb moisture from the marshmallows and the surrounding air. Using the gluten-free range of these cookies may help them stay crisp for longer.

Sprinkles

Sprinkles add colour and texture to marshmallows. Single coloured non pareil sprinkles may be used to give marshmallows a "furry look" without the need for functional dusting. In this book, I also use individual pieces to decorate my creations. See page 41 for more details.

Adding Fine Details on Marshmallows

There are various ingredients and tools that can be used to add fine details on cured marshmallows. This includes facial features and decorative details that may be too fine or time-consuming to add using marshmallow batter.

Melted Chocolate

Melted dark chocolate is an excellent choice for adding fine facial features like stubby noses and beady eyes on character marshmallows as it does not smudge or dissolve. Melted white chocolate can be coloured with oil-based food colouring if coloured features are required. Melt the chocolate with a little vegetable shortening or oil using the microwave oven or by double-boiling. Use 20 parts chocolate to 1 part vegetable shortening (by weight). Transfer into an OPP cone for piping. Alternatively, a skewer can also be used to draw details.

Gel Food Colouring

Painting fine features like eyebrows and smiles can be done using a very fine brush and gel food colouring. Note however that gel straight from the bottle is too wet and the colours will bleed if the marshmallows are left to sit. To get around this, thicken the gel by dropping a few drops onto a palette and leaving it to air-dry for several days. To use, moisten a fine brush with a little water and dab off the excess. Pick up the air-dried gel with the moistened brush. Ensure the marshmallows have been cured overnight to minimise spreading of the paint. Dust the marshmallows after painting.

Lustre Dust

Lustre dust is a type of powdered food colouring that can be applied in its dry form with a brush. Lustre dust in different shades of pink is often used to create rosy cheeks on character marshmallows. A little goes a long way so remember to knock off the excess powder from the brush before applying on cured marshmallows. Apply additional coats to deepen the shade gradually as it would be difficult to erase if too much was applied initially. Lustre dust may be applied before or after dusting the cured marshmallows.

Sprinkles

Sprinkles with unique designs can be used to decorate marshmallow creations, such as stars on Christmas trees. Chocolate non pareil sprinkles or mini chocolate Crispearls can be used as eyes and noses as an alternative to melted chocolate. As sprinkles are small in size, use tweezers to handle them. Attach sprinkles to cured marshmallows before dusting.

Storing Marshmallows

Marshmallows made with regular sugar that have been dusted or coated should be stored in airtight conditions. They will keep for up to 2 weeks at cool room temperature (18°C–25°C). Store the marshmallows immediately to keep them fresh and prevent them from drying out.

If planning to toast gelatine-based marshmallows, leave them to air-dry for 2–4 days to ensure that they hold their shape well when toasted. Marshmallows made with allulose should be stored in airtight conditions in the refrigerator. Marshmallows with chocolate ganache, white chocolate and gelatine-based fillings may be stored in the fridge after 3 days and up to 2 weeks to ensure that the fillings stay fresh without drying out the marshmallows too much.

There are several ways to keep marshmallows in airtight conditions. For home consumption, line the base of the airtight container with paper towels followed by baking paper. The paper towel will absorb any moisture and keep the air in the container dry. A desiccant can also be used. In cool and dry environments, marshmallows can be stored stacked in the container. In hot and humid environments, dust the marshmallows with a little extra cornstarch to prevent sticking. Store the marshmallows in layers separated by baking paper.

If packing marshmallows as party favours, use heat-seal bags or small resealable bags. If the environment is hot and humid, store gelatine-based marshmallows in the freezer until needed, store agar-based marshmallows in an air-conditioned room until needed. Do not freeze agar-based marshmallows as it will change the texture. Since agar-based marshmallows cannot be frozen, do not make them too far in advance. Consume within 2 weeks.

Store gelatine-based marshmallows in an airtight container in the freezer if keeping for more than 2 weeks or if the environment is very warm (27°C and above). Gelatine-based marshmallows can be kept in the freezer for several months. When ready to consume, leave the marshmallows in the airtight container and bring to room temperature before opening. This will prevent condensation from forming on the marshmallows, causing them to become sticky.

Marshmallow Fillings

Fillings add another dimension to the taste and texture of marshmallows. Choose fillings that complement the marshmallow in terms of flavour and design, and avoid fillings that have a high water content as they will dissolve the surrounding marshmallow.

The fillings in this book can be set in two ways: (1) in silicone moulds if you want them in specific shapes or (2) in homemade trays made out of aluminium foil, lined with parchment. The set filling can then be cut out using cookie cutters or a small knife into circles, squares, rectangles or other shapes.

Dark Chocolate Ganache with Variations

Feel free to adjust the ratio of ingredients according to climate and taste.

Dark Chocolate Ganache

200 g dark chocolate couverture

100 g butter (salted or unsalted), heavy cream OR a combination of both

1 tsp vanilla bean paste or extract

Optional Flavours

½ tsp peppermint extract or 2–3 drops peppermint oil (adjusted according to strength of flavouring)

1–2 tsp instant coffee granules, dissolved in 30 g heavy cream

½–1 tsp pumpkin spice

1. Place all ingredients in a heatproof bowl. Set it over a saucepan of barely simmering water. Stir with spatula to melt the chocolate until smooth. Alternatively, place all ingredients in a microwaveable bowl. Heat the chocolate using medium power for 10 seconds and stir with a spatula. Repeat until the chocolate is melted and smooth. Do not rush the process to avoid overheating the chocolate.

2. Pour into prepared aluminium foil tray or into a piping bag and pipe into silicone hemisphere moulds. Refrigerate until firm. This takes 30 minutes to 1 hour. You may prepare this ahead of time.

3. Unmould or cut individual portions of filling and place on a lined tray. Refrigerate until needed.

Variation

If making coffee dark chocolate ganache, add 30 g warm heavy cream to dissolve the instant coffee granules before adding to the chocolate.

Pour ganache into prepared aluminium foil tray or into a piping bag and pipe into silicone moulds. Refrigerate until firm. This will take about 2 hours but you may prepare this ahead of time.

Unmould or cut the individual portions of filling and place on a lined tray. Refrigerate until needed.

Brigadeiros

This is a delightful Brazilian version of chocolate caramel fudge.

1. Melt the butter in a heavy saucepan over medium heat. Add condensed milk and cocoa powder. Stir continuously with a spatula until the base of the saucepan is visible for 2–3 seconds when a spatula is pulled across the pan.

2. Pour into greased silicone moulds and set in the fridge. Alternatively, pour onto a greased plate and refrigerate for an hour.

3. Portion out 10 g chilled mixture and roll into balls. Leave as it is or coat with sprinkles, cocoa powder or chopped nuts. Place on a lined tray and refrigerate until needed.

260 g sweetened condensed milk

20 g cocoa powder

10 g butter (salted or unsalted)

Chocolate sprinkles, cocoa powder, finely chopped nuts (optional coating)

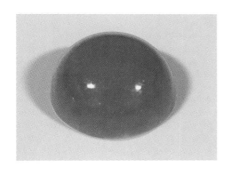

Salted Caramel

1. Grease silicone moulds lightly with softened butter. Alternatively, line an 18-cm square and grease.

2. Melt butter in a heavy bottomed saucepan over medium heat.

3. In a medium bowl, combine sugar, salt, corn syrup and condensed milk.

4. When butter is fully melted, add condensed milk mixture. Turn heat up to medium-high and cook until mixture starts to boil.

5. Lower heat to medium. Monitor temperature using a candy thermometer. Stir constantly until temperature reaches 120°C.

6. Remove from heat and stir in vanilla. Be careful as the mixture will bubble rapidly.

7. Pour carefully into prepared moulds or a lined pan. Refrigerate overnight to firm up caramel if the environment is warm.

8. Unmould or cut filling and place on a tray lined with baking paper. Refrigerate until needed.

75 g unsalted butter

170 g light brown sugar

2 tsp sea salt

110 g light corn syrup

130 g sweetened condensed milk

1 tsp vanilla extract or paste

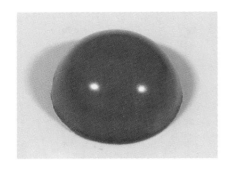

White Chocolate and Gelatine-Based Filling with Tea

The amount of white chocolate and gelatine used can be adjusted according to the climate. Use less gelatine and/or white chocolate if the recipe below is too firm for your liking.

Tea Flavours

48 g chilled brewed tea (*see* Note) or ice water

12 g gelatine powder

120 g white chocolate couverture

60 g brewed tea (*see* Note) or milk

30 g unsalted butter

⅛ tsp salt

18 g tea powder (*see* Note)

6 g dried tea leaves/flowers (*see* Note), finely ground and sifted

Note: Tea-flavoured fillings can be made from two sources of tea:

(1) Infusions from dried leaves/flowers. Steep 8 teabags/16 g tea leaves/flowers in 160 g boiling water for 10 minutes. Squeeze all water from teabag/tea leaves/flowers. Cover and refrigerate tea until cold. Part of it will be used for blooming gelatine. Grind and sift about 6 g dried tea leaves/flowers and set aside. Add to melted chocolate and gelatine mixture to boost tea flavour. Adjust amount of tea leaves/flowers added according to strength of tea.

(2) Milk tea from dissolving tea powder in warm milk. Whisk 18 g tea powder in 60 g warm milk until dissolved. Strain to remove any stubborn lumps in the tea.

1. Bloom gelatine in 48 g chilled brewed tea or ice water. Set aside for 10 minutes.

2. Place white chocolate in a microwaveable bowl. Heat on medium power for 10 seconds and stir. Repeat until slightly softened. It does not need to be melted.

3. Place 60 g brewed tea or 78 g milk tea, butter and salt in a small microwaveable bowl. Heat until butter is melted and mixture is warm.

4. Melt bloomed gelatine in a microwave oven at medium power for 10 seconds. Stir until gelatine is melted. Add melted gelatine to melted butter mixture. Stir and mix until well combined.

5. Pour mixture into softened white chocolate and let sit for 30 seconds. Stir until white chocolate is melted. Heat briefly in the microwave or over a pot of barely simmering water if there are bits of unmelted chocolate. Be careful not to overheat or the chocolate will seize. Add 6 g finely ground tea leaves/flowers if desired and mix well.

6. Pour into prepared aluminium foil tray or into a piping bag and then pipe into silicone hemisphere moulds. Refrigerate until set firm. About 2 hours but you may prepare this ahead of time.

7. Unmould or cut individual portions of filling and place on a lined tray. Refrigerate until needed.

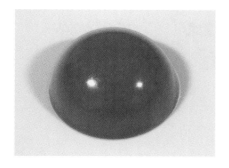

White Chocolate and Gelatine-Based Filling with Coffee

1. Follow the same steps as for tea but replace brewed tea with brewed coffee and make milk coffee by dissolving instant coffee granules in warm milk. Adjust the strength of the coffee according to taste. For reference, I replaced 18 g tea powder with 8 g instant coffee granules.

White Chocolate and Gelatine-Based Filling with Fruit and Berries

Use strawberries, raspberries, blueberries, blackberries or a combination of fruit and berries. It does not matter if they are fresh or frozen. It will taste just as good!

60 g chilled berry jam
  (*see* Note)

12 g gelatine powder

100 g white chocolate couverture

40 g berry jam (*see* Note)

30 g unsalted butter

⅛ tsp salt

1–2 tsp strawberry paste (optional)

Note: To make berry jam, blend berries and sieve. Sieving is optional. Do it only if you prefer not to have skins and pips in the filling. Add sugar (10% weight of blended berries or to taste), a pinch of salt and 1 tsp lemon juice. Cook in saucepan over low heat until reduced to 60% of the original weight.

1. Follow the same steps as for tea but replace brewed tea with berry jam. Add strawberry paste, if using, to the berry jam and butter mixture before melting.

White Chocolate and Gelatine-Based Filling with Sour Citrus

Sour citrus fruits like yuzu, lemon and lime can be made into a refreshing filling that offsets the sweetness of marshmallows. Use freshly-squeezed juice or 100% juice from a bottle. Fruit zest or peel can be added to boost the flavour.

1. Follow the same steps as for as tea but replace brewed tea with citrus juice. Add candied peel or zest to the melted mixture before pouring into moulds/trays.

60 g chilled citrus juice

12 g gelatine powder

120 g white chocolate couverture

30 g milk

30 g unsalted butter

⅛ tsp salt

1 Tbsp finely chopped candied peel or zest

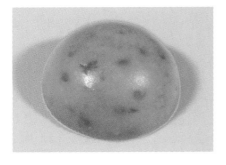

White Chocolate and Gelatine-Based Filling with Nut Butters

Marshmallows that encase nut butter or have it swirled in are usually made without egg whites. As Italian meringue-based marshmallows contain egg whites, it will not adhere to the nut butter filling. The nut butter may also cause the marshmallow to deflate due to its fat content. To get around this, I Incorporate the nut butter into a white chocolate and gelatine base. Make your own nut butter or use store-bought ones. Adjust with salt according to taste. Add chopped roasted nuts for texture if desired.

1. Follow the same steps as for tea flavours but replace brewed tea with ice water and unsalted butter with nut butter. Add chopped nuts to the melted mixture before setting in moulds/trays.

45 g ice water

9–12 g gelatine powder (*see* Note)

120 g white chocolate couverture

60 g milk

90 g creamy nut butter (*see* Note)

¼ tsp salt (optional)

30 g chopped nuts (optional)

Note: Use more gelatine powder if the nut butter is runny. If making your own nut butter, begin by roasting nuts in the oven at 160°C for 10 minutes or until lightly browned and fragrant. Pulse in the blender with a little oil and salt to taste.

Mung bean paste

Azuki bean paste

White Chocolate and Gelatine-Based Filling with Bean Pastes

Marshmallows filled with bean pastes are reminiscent of Asian desserts like *ang ku kueh* or azuki bean mochi. As store-bought pastes are often loaded with sugar, they may not be suitable. Unsweetened homemade pastes take some time and effort but it will be worth it.

1. Follow the same steps as for tea flavours but replace brewed tea with bean purée. Add 1–2 tsp cold water to bloomed gelatine in cold bean purée if mixture of 100 g bean purée and gelatine seems dry and feels gritty between your fingers.

100 g cold bean purée (see Note)

10 g gelatine powder

80 g white chocolate couverture

40 g bean purée (*see* Note)

20 g unsalted butter

¼–½ tsp salt or to taste

1–2 tsp cold water as necessary

Note: To make bean paste, rinse and drain 150 g dried beans. Place washed beans in a large steaming plate and cover with 300–400 g water. Add 2–3 knotted pandan leaves and steam for 1½ hours or until soft. Add more water if necessary. The beans are sufficiently steamed when you are able to mash a bean between your fingers easily. Purée in blender. Press steamed beans through a fine sieve, if desired. This removes the skins and makes the paste smoother. Excess bean purée can be wrapped with cling film and stored in the freezer.

Frequently Asked Questions
Gelatine-Based Marshmallows

Sticky Even After Dusting

Why are my marshmallows sticky even after dusting?

a) The temperature of the sugar syrup was too low. Check the accuracy of the thermometer used by testing the temperature of boiling water. It should be 100°C if you are at sea level. Adjust accordingly if you live at higher altitudes.

b) There was not enough gelatine added. This is likely if you are working with a highly acidic bloom liquid. Increase the amount of gelatine added to compensate for the loss in gelling strength.

c) The environment is very humid. Dust using only cornstarch and use two coats instead of one. Store immediately in an airtight container.

Deflate Over Time

Why do my marshmallows deflate some time after I pipe?

a) The marshmallow batter was not sufficiently whipped before piping. You may need to whip at a higher speed setting or whip for a longer time before or after adding melted gelatine to the egg whites.

b) The syrup temperature was too low. Check the accuracy of the thermometer used.

c) The type of gelatine used is not suited for your environment. For example, fish gelatine does not work well in environments above 24°C.

Batter Set Too Quickly

My marshmallow batter set too quickly for me to complete piping all my marshmallows. How do I go about working?

Microwave the piping bag of hardened marshmallow at medium power for 3 seconds. Massage the bag a little and continue working. Note that you can only microwave the piping bag once or twice. It is not advisable to microwave it more than twice as the meringue structure will break down with each round. The gelling properties of gelatine will also be affected.

Try not to up-size the recipes. Work with small portions each time. Work in a warmer environment if possible. If not, reduce the amount of gelatine by 1 g. If you are working in a cool climate, use fish gelatine instead of bovine or porcine gelatine. Divide the marshmallow batter into multiple piping bags and keep the unused bags on a heating pad or on a baking tray in a warm oven (27°C–30°C). Leave the oven light on to create a warm environment in the oven. Alternatively, place a container of hot water in the oven.

Colours Run During Storage

Why do the colours seem to run during storage?

a) Too much gel food colouring was used. As food colours deepen with storage time, go for a slightly lighter shade than you want to minimise the amount of colouring used.

b) There was too much moisture in the marshmallow batter/gel food colouring. Bring the sugar syrup to a higher temperature before pouring into the egg whites or use less liquid for blooming gelatine. Do not add too much water to thin out the marshmallow batter or food gel colouring when adding fine facial features. The additional moisture will cause the gel colouring to spread.

c) There was condensation on the surface of the marshmallows. If the marshmallows were stored in the fridge or freezer, make sure to leave them in the closed container until they are at room temperature before opening to prevent condensation from forming on the surface of the marshmallows.

Batter Does Not Set

My marshmallows don't seem to set and they remain wet and sticky.

a) There is too much water content in the marshmallows. This could be due to a syrup temperature that was too low.

b) The gel strength of the gelatine was reduced or too low. Use more gelatine and/or use gelatine with higher bloom strength.

Batter Becomes Runny

Why does my marshmallow batter become runny in the stand mixer while whipping?

This can happen when the added ingredients contain fat, such as oil-based flavouring/emulsions.

Grainy Bits

Why are there grainy bits in my marshmallows?

This is likely due to gelatine powder that was not fully hydrated or melted. Make sure that the gelatine is correctly bloomed and that all the granules are moistened when mixing gelatine powder with cold liquid. Make sure that the bloomed gelatine is fully melted before adding to the Italian meringue.

Agar-Based Marshmallows

Batter Became Grainy

Why did my marshmallow batter become grainy after adding the agar syrup?

This happens when the agar syrup is added to the meringue too quickly. Pour the syrup slowly down the side of the bowl to avoid this.

Batter Set Too Quickly

My marshmallow batter set too quickly for me to complete piping all my marshmallows. How do I go about working?

Agar-based marshmallows set a lot faster than gelatine-based marshmallows so it is a good idea not to be too ambitious with each batch. Keep to one or two colours in a single batch. Unlike gelatine-based marshmallows, agar-based marshmallows that have set in the piping bag cannot be salvaged by microwaving. Make sure everything is prepared and laid out before you begin making the marshmallows. The following steps will also help keep the marshmallow at a pipeable consistency for a longer time:

a) Divide the marshmallow batter into multiple piping bags and keep the unused bags on a heating pad or on a baking tray in a warm oven (27°C–30°C). Leave the oven light on to create a warm environment in the oven. Alternatively, place a container of hot water in the oven.

b) Keep unused marshmallow batter in the stand mixer bowl and whip at the lowest speed to prevent it from setting.

c) Work in a warmer environment.

d) Cook the agar syrup to a slightly lower temperature to keep the water content slightly higher, but not too much.

e) Whip the marshmallow batter for a shorter time so the consistency is less stiff when you begin to pipe.

Note: Do not overdo (d) and (e) or you may have difficulty drying the marshmallows.

When Agar Syrup Is Ready

I have difficulty monitoring the temperature of the agar syrup. How do I know when it is ready?

Gauge the readiness of the syrup by monitoring the consistency. Make sure you are able to produce threads of agar syrup for at least 1 minute when the whisk is lifted before removing from the heat.

Marshmallows Not Set

Why are my marshmallows not set even after leaving out to dry for two days?

The water content of the marshmallow batter is too high. This could be due to undercooking the agar syrup or the fruit jam containing too much moisture. Very humid environments are not conducive for agar-based marshmallows. Trying using 1–2 g more agar, especially if the bloom strength of the agar you are using is unknown.

Marshmallows Weep

Why do my marshmallows weep during storage?

a) The fruit jam contains too much moisture. This may be more of an issue when adding fruit with a high water content to the apple purée. This is why I recommend baking the apples instead of steaming when making apple purée for the jam.

b) The meringue was under-whipped when the agar syrup was added.

c) The marshmallow batter was under-whipped before transferring to the piping bag.

Surface Is Rough

Why is the surface of my marshmallows rough?

The marshmallow batter could have been over-beaten or it was left in the piping bag for too long such that it started to set before the mixture was piped.

Pretty Awesome

Rose and Tulip Marshmallows

Makes 35 marshmallows

Marshmallow

1 portion agar-based marshmallow
  batter (page 24 or 29)

Strawberry emulco or pink gel
  food colouring

½ tsp matcha powder

1–2 drops green gel food colouring
  (optional)

Suggested Dusting

Icing sugar, cornstarch or any
  preferred functional dusting of
  choice (page 37)

> ### Variations
>
> Make mango or passionfruit
> marshmallow batter (page 33).
> Add some yellow gel food
> colouring for yellow flowers.

Scan the QR code to
view a video tutorial on
piping roses and tulips.

1. Prepare 6-cm squares of baking paper, one for each rose. Line baking tray for tulips. Prepare a large piping bag fitted with a petal tip (#125) for roses, a large piping bag fitted with a tulip Russian piping tip (#242) for tulips, and a small piping bag fitted with a leaf tip of choice. I used tips #68 and #352. Prepare another small piping bag without a tip.

2. Prepare marshmallow batter. Portion out 40 g into a small microwaveable bowl, add matcha powder and mix well. Add green gel food colouring if desired. Cover bowl with cling wrap and leave in a warm oven with the light on until you are ready to pipe leaves.

3. Divide remaining batter into 2 equal portions. Transfer 1 portion into a piping bag fitted with a tulip tip. Keep other portion covered with cling wrap in warm oven.

4. Pipe tulips. Keep them about 8 cm apart for piping leaves.

5. Add strawberry emulco or pink gel food colouring to remaining batter to colour it pink. Transfer about 30 g pink batter into a small piping bag without a piping tip and the rest into large piping bad fitted with a petal tip.

6. Pipe roses. Attach a square of baking paper to a flower nail with a little marshmallow batter. Cut a 1-cm hole in the small piping bag and pipe a cone about 3–4-cm tall. Pipe centre of rose using petal tip with the narrow end of tip facing upwards. Rotate flower nail as you apply constant pressure on the piping bag to create spiral for centre of rose centre. Pipe 3 petals around rose centre. Stop here for rose buds or pipe another layer of 5 petals over the 3 petals for a larger rose. Carefully remove from flower nail and place on a baking tray.

7. Stir green batter with spatula until it is smooth again. Transfer to a piping bag fitted with a leaf tip. Pipe 2-3 leaves up the sides of each tulip. Pipe leaves up the sides of roses or as separate pieces on baking paper.

8. Leave piped marshmallows to dry overnight or for at least 8 hours.

9. Dust and peel flowers (and leaves) off baking paper.

10. Arrange as desired or store in airtight containers at cool room temperature. Consume within 2 weeks. Store sugar-free marshmallows in the fridge.

Jack-O'-Lantern Marshmallows

Makes about 20 marshmallows

Marshmallow

1 portion basic agar-based
  marshmallow batter (page 24 or
  29); apple purée replaced with
  pumpkin purée (page 34)

Orange or pumpkin gel food
  colouring

Suggested Filling

Dark chocolate ganache (page 44)
  or white chocolate and gelatine-
  based filling with coffee (page 47)

½–1 tsp pumpkin spice

Suggested Dusting

Icing sugar, cornstarch or any
  preferred functional dusting of
  choice (page 37)

Finishing

Chocolate chip

Melted dark chocolate

Black cocoa powder, charcoal
  powder or black oil-based
  food colouring

1. Prepare 6-cm squares of baking paper, one for each pumpkin. Trace a 3-cm circle on each square using a pencil. Prepare 1–2 large piping bags fitted with tip #12, depending on how fast you work. Use one bag at a time if you work slowly, stirring batter until smooth before transferring into piping bag. Keep any unused batter covered in a warm oven with the light on.

2. Prepare filling of choice and pipe into 3-cm silicone hemisphere moulds. Mix in pumpkin spice if desired and leave to set. Unmould filling and place on a lined tray. Keep refrigerated until ready to assemble.

3. Prepare marshmallow batter. Add orange or pumpkin gel colouring to achieve desired shade. Transfer to prepared piping bag.

4. Pipe pumpkins. Attach a square of baking paper, pencilled-side down, on a flower nail with a little marshmallow batter. Pipe a 3-cm wide x 1-cm thick disc. Place a portion of filling on piped batter. Pipe radial lines of batter starting from base of filling and moving upwards, releasing pressure on piping bag as you pipe. Rotate flower nail with each new radial line until filling is fully encased. Carefully remove from flower nail and place on a baking tray.

5. Leave piped marshmallows to dry overnight or for at least 8 hours.

6. Dust and peel pumpkins off baking paper.

7. Press a chocolate chip into the top of each pumpkin to make an indent. Use a small brush to apply a little water on indent, then attach a chocolate chip to moistened indent.

8. Colour melted dark chocolate black using black cocoa powder, charcoal powder or black oil-based food colouring. Transfer to an OPP cone and pipe eyes and mouths. Let chocolate set fully.

9. Store in airtight containers at cool room temperature for up to 3 days or in the fridge for up to 2 weeks. Store sugar-free marshmallows in the fridge.

Christmas Tree Marshmallows

Makes 30–35 marshmallows

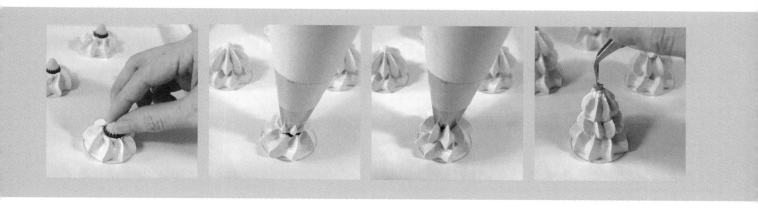

Marshmallow

1 portion basic agar-based
  marshmallow batter (page 24
  or 29);

1–1.5 tsp pandan paste

1–2 drops green gel food colouring
  (optional)

Suggested Dusting

Icing sugar, cornstarch or any
  preferred functional dusting of
  choice (page 37)

Finishing

Star sprinkles

Strawberry chocolate candy

White nonpareils sprinkles
  (optional)

1. Prepare marshmallow batter. Add pandan paste and gel food colouring to agar syrup before boiling.

2. Prepare baking tray with 4-cm circle template (page 130).

3. Prepare a large piping bag fitted with a large open star tip. I used tip #827. Transfer batter into piping bag.

4. Pipe bottom tier of tree. Hold piping tip above centre of circle and squeeze piping bag until batter fills circle. Release pressure and lift piping tip.

5. Place a candy in the middle of bottom tier, if desired, pressing it firmly into the batter. Place piping tip over candy such that half the candy is in the tip. Apply pressure on piping bag to pipe middle tier. Ensure batter fully encases candy before lifting off.

6. Position tip over middle tier and apply pressure on piping bag to pipe top tier. Finish by releasing pressure on piping bag and giving it a quick jerk upwards.

7. Place a star sprinkle at the top of each tree. Decorate with white nonpareil sprinkles if desired. Leave piped marshmallows to dry overnight or for at least 8 hours.

8. Dust and peel trees off baking paper.

9. Store in airtight containers at cool room temperature and consume within 2 weeks. Store sugar-free marshmallows in the fridge.

Hydrangea Marshmallows

Makes about 12 marshmallows

Marshmallow

1 portion basic agar-based
marshmallow batter (page 24
or 29); 100 g apple purée
replaced with 70 g berry purée
and 70 g apple purée (page 33)

Royal blue and purple gel food
colouring

Suggested Dusting

Icing sugar, cornstarch or any
preferred functional dusting of
choice (page 37)

Suggested Filling

Chocolate and hazelnut
confection

Variations

Make mango or
passionfruit marshmallow
batter (page 33). Leave
half the batter uncoloured
and colour the other half
with a little green gel food
colouring for another
colour of hydrangeas.

1. Prepare 8-cm squares of baking paper, one for each hydrangea cluster. Trace out a 4-cm circle on each square using a pencil. Prepare 2 large piping bags fitted with tip #2D.

2. Prepare marshmallow batter and divide into 2 portions. Colour one blue and the other purple.

3. Use a small spatula to stripe blue and purple marshmallow batters, alternating colours in the piping bag. Cover any remaining batter with cling wrap and fill second bag only after first bag is empty. Stir batter until smooth again before filling second bag.

4. Attach a square of baking paper, pencilled-side down, on a flower nail with a little marshmallow batter. Pipe a 4-cm wide and 1-cm thick disc.

5. Place chocolate confection on piped batter.

6. Form hydrangea by piping a ring of florets around the base of chocolate. To pipe a floret, apply pressure on the piping bag while rotating the piping tip. Release pressure on the bag and give it a quick jerk away from the surface. Pipe another ring of florets above the first ring. Complete hydrangea by piping a floret on top. Try not to leave any gaps between florets. For a larger bunch of hydrangeas, pipe another layer, but work quickly. Carefully remove from flower nail and place on a baking tray.

7. Leave piped marshmallows to dry overnight or for at least 8 hours.

8. Dust and peel hydrangeas off baking paper. Hydrangeas can be arranged with other flowers and leaves (page 56) to form a bouquet.

9. Store in airtight containers at cool room temperature and consume within 2 weeks. Store sugar-free marshmallows in the fridge.

Acorn Marshmallows

Makes 25–30 marshmallows

Marshmallow

1 portion basic agar-based marshmallow batter (page 24 or 29), flavoured with tea or coffee (page 34)

Orange gel food colouring

Yellow gel food colouring

Brown and espresso gel food colouring

$\frac{1}{8}$ tsp charcoal powder

Suggested Dusting and Coating

Icing sugar, cornstarch or any preferred functional dusting of choice (page 37)

Chocolate rice sprinkles

Finishing

Dark chocolate

Black cocoa powder, charcoal powder or black oil-based food colouring

White chocolate

Pink powder or oil-based food colouring

1. Prepare baking tray with 3.5-cm circle template (page 132) for acorn cupules and another baking tray with 3-cm circle template for acorn nuts (page 132).

2. Prepare 2 large piping bags, each fitted with a large round tip. I used a 2.4-cm round tip for piping nuts and tip #808 for piping cupules. Prepare a small piping bag fitted with tip #7 or #8.

3. Prepare marshmallow batter. Whip batter for 2–2½ minutes or until batter starts to show signs of peeling away from sides of bowl for a slightly softer piping consistency. Add yellow, orange and brown colouring until desired light brown shade is achieved. Transfer into prepared large piping bag with 2.4-cm round tip. Portion out 140 g batter, cover with cling wrap and set aside in a warm oven with the light on.

4. Pipe 3–3.5-cm high mounds for nuts using light brown batter. Apply constant pressure on piping bag while moving the tip upwards at a constant speed. To end off, release pressure on piping bag while giving it a quick twirl. Tap down any peaks with a damp finger.

5. Add charcoal powder and yellow, orange, espresso and brown colouring to reserved batter until shade matches colour of chocolate rice sprinkles. Transfer into prepared large piping bag fitted with tip #808. Pipe 1.5-cm mounds for cupules. Transfer remaining batter into prepared small piping bag. Pipe stems on cupules.

6. Leave piped marshmallows to dry overnight or for at least 8 hours.

7. Dust nuts with functional dusting of choice. Scatter and press chocolate rice sprinkles into cupules with gloved hands.

8. Peel nuts and cupules off baking paper without dusting bases. Stick cupules on nuts. Gently press rim of cupules to match base of nuts.

9. Melt dark chocolate and add black cocoa powder, charcoal powder or black oil-based colouring to colour it black. Melt white chocolate and colour a portion pink with powder or oil-based colouring. Transfer into OPP cones and pipe features. Let chocolate set fully.

10. Store in airtight containers at cool room temperature and consume within 2 weeks. Store sugar-free marshmallows in the fridge.

Xiao Long Bao Marshmallows

Makes about 18 marshmallows

Marshmallow

1 portion basic gelatine-based
  marshmallow batter (page 20
  or 28)

3 pandan leaves, washed and
  cut into 3-cm lengths (optional)

300 g water (optional)

Pink gel food colouring

Charcoal powder or black gel
  food colouring

A little warm water as needed

Suggested Dusting

Cornstarch or any preferred
  functional dusting of choice
  (page 37)

Suggested Filling

Mung bean, red bean (page 49)
  or any filling of choice
  (page 44)

1. Prepare baking tray with 3-cm circle template (page 132).

2. Prepare filling of choice and set it in 3-cm silicone hemisphere moulds. Unmould filling and place on a lined tray. Keep refrigerated until ready to assemble.

3. Prepare marshmallow batter with a slightly stiffer consistency. Heat syrup to 117°C–119°C. Whip Italian meringue for 3 minutes or until the meringue consistently peels off the sides of the mixing bowl before adding gelatine. Beat marshmallow batter for 3–4 minutes until firm peaks form. If using mung bean or red bean filling, use pandan water for blooming gelatine and for the syrup. Boil 3 pandan leaves in 300 g water for 10 minutes. Strain. Chill some pandan water for blooming gelatine.

4. Transfer 30 g marshmallow batter into a small piping bag and cut a 3-mm hole cut at the tip. Transfer rest of batter into a large piping bag fitted with a large round tip. I used tip #808.

5. Using the large piping bag, pipe 1–1.5-cm high discs on baking tray. Freeze for 2 minutes.

6. Use a skewer to scratch crosshatch lines on the base of filling. Place a hemisphere of filling on each disc. Use a skewer to scratch domed surface of filling. You may also scratch domed surface before placing filling on piped marshmallow batter. Scratching the surface of the filling helps it to adhere to the marshmallow. Position piping tip 1–1.5 cm away from top of filling. Apply constant pressure on piping bag and pipe until batter covers both filling and disc. Release pressure on piping bag and lift off.

7. Insert tip of small piping bag into top of *bao* and apply constant pressure as you move the bag upwards by about 1 cm. Release pressure and give the bag a quick jerk upwards. Pipe a small ring to form 'pleats' at the top of each bao.

8. Portion out about 2 tsp white batter and colour it black using charcoal powder or black gel food colouring. Add warm water one drop at a time to thin consistency of batter a little. Microwave to soften if necessary.

9. Portion out about 1 tsp white batter and colour it pink. Pipe or paint features on bao. Use OPP cones if piping and a fine brush or skewer if painting.

10. Refrigerate piped marshmallows for 30 minutes to 2 hours or overnight in an air-conditioned room. Dust and dislodge marshmallows from baking paper.

11. Store in airtight containers at cool room temperature for up to 3 days or in the fridge for up to 2 weeks. Store sugar-free marshmallows in the fridge

Watermelon Marshmallows

Makes about 12 marshmallows (before cutting)

Marshmallow

1 portion basic gelatine-based marshmallow batter (page 20 or 28)

½–1 tsp strawberry emulco

½–1 tsp pandan paste

Red and green gel colouring (optional)

Suggested Dusting

Cornstarch or any preferred functional dusting of choice (page 37)

Finishing

Melted dark chocolate

1. Spray inside of cupcake cases with non-stick spray or grease with melted butter or oil. Alternatively, use silicone cupcake moulds. I used 6-cm diameter cupcake cases.

2. Prepare marshmallow batter. Portion out 35 g batter into a small piping bag fitted with tip #8.

3. Portion out 120 g batter and add pandan paste. Mix well and transfer into a large piping bag fitted with tip #12.

4. Add strawberry emulco to remaining marshmallow batter. Mix well and transfer into a large piping bag. Cut an 8–10-mm hole at the tip.

5. Pipe a ring of green batter, tracing the circumference of the cupcake cases/moulds. Immediately pipe a ring of white batter next to the green batter. Fill middle of white ring with red batter. Tap down any peaks.

6. Refrigerate piped marshmallows for 30 minutes to 2 hours or overnight in an air-conditioned room.

7. Fill a small tray with dusting of choice. Carefully peel away cupcake cases/moulds and drop marshmallows onto dusting. Coat well with dusting and toss in a sieve to remove excess dusting.

8. To create halves and wedges, freeze dusted marshmallows for 30 minutes, then cut using a lightly greased knife. Clean and grease the knife after each cut. Dust cut surfaces of marshmallows.

9. Pipe or paint watermelon seeds on slices using melted dark chocolate. Let chocolate set fully.

10. Store in airtight containers at cool room temperature and consume within 2 weeks. Store sugar-free marshmallows in the fridge.

Rainbow Marshmallows

Makes about 20 marshmallows

Marshmallow

1 portion basic gelatine-based marshmallow batter (page 20 or 28), flavoured with sour citrus (page 30)

Red, yellow, green and blue gel food colouring

Suggested Dusting

Cornstarch or any preferred functional dusting of choice (page 37)

1. Prepare baking trays with rainbow and cloud templates (page 133).

2. Prepare marshmallow batter. Portion out 20 g marshmallow batter for each rainbow colour. Add colouring one drop at a time until the desired shade is achieved. Transfer into small piping bags and cut a 3-mm hole at the tip.

3. Pipe rainbows in this order — red, yellow, green and blue — for half the rainbows and the reverse order for the other half. Place rainbows in the freezer for 10–15 minutes while piping clouds.

4. Transfer about 180 g white batter into a large piping bag and cut a 1-cm hole at the tip. Pipe a series of blobs as outlined by the template to create clouds. Place clouds in the freezer for 10 minutes.

5. Dust and dislodge rainbows from baking paper after they have come to room temperature.

6. Remove clouds from freezer. Pipe blobs of white marshmallow where the ends of the rainbow should go. Freeze for 2 minutes. Carefully place a rainbow upright on a cloud, leaning slightly into the two supports at the rainbow ends. When rainbow is secure, pipe small blobs of white marshmallow batter in the front as well.

7. Refrigerate piped marshmallows for 30 minutes to 2 hours or overnight in an air-conditioned room.

8. Dust and dislodge marshmallows from baking paper.

9. Store in airtight containers at cool room temperature and consume within 2 weeks. Store sugar-free marshmallows in the fridge.

Pineapple Tart Marshmallows

Makes 20–24 marshmallows

Marshmallow

1 portion basic gelatine-based marshmallow batter (page 20 or 28), flavoured with reduced fresh or 100% canned pineapple juice (page 30)

Yellow, ivory and orange gel food colouring

1 tsp warm water

Suggested Dusting

Cornstarch or any preferred functional dusting of choice (page 37)

1. Prepare baking trays with 4.5-cm circle template (page 131).

2. Prepare marshmallow batter with stiff consistency. Heat syrup to 120°C–125°C. Whip Italian meringue for 3 minutes or until meringue consistently peels off the sides of the mixing bowl before adding gelatine. Beat marshmallow batter until melted gelatine is thoroughly incorporated, about 1½-3 minutes.

3. Add yellow and ivory colouring so batter resembles tart pastry.

4. Transfer 25 g batter into a small microwaveable bowl. Cover with cling wrap and set aside. Transfer about 180 g batter into a large piping bag fitted with a large French star tip. I used tip #868.

5. Add warm water ¼ tsp at a time to remaining batter and mix well until batter reaches a floppy peak consistency. Cover with cling wrap and set aside for making pineapple filling.

6. Pipe tart pastry bases by twisting large piping bag with star tip while applying pressure on piping bag. Release pressure on bag before lifting off once batter fills circle template. Tap down any peaks. Refrigerate while preparing pineapple filling.

7. Prepare pineapple filling. Add orange and ivory colouring to batter and mix well. Transfer to a piping bag fitted with a round tip. I used tip #807.

8. Remove chilled trays of tart pastry base from fridge. Pipe mounds of pineapple filling on pastry bases. Tap down any peaks. Refrigerate while preparing pastry topping.

9. Microwave reserved 25 g marshmallow batter for 3 seconds on medium power. Add ⅛ tsp warm water and mix well. Repeat heating until batter is at a pipeable consistency. Transfer into a piping bag fitted with tip #5.

10. Remove chilled trays of marshmallows from fridge. Pipe a short horizontal line across the top of each pineapple filling, then pipe a short vertical line to form a cross.

11. Refrigerate piped marshmallows for 30 minutes to 2 hours or overnight in an air-conditioned room.

12. Dust and dislodge marshmallows from baking paper.

13. Store in airtight containers at cool room temperature and consume within 2 weeks. Store sugar-free marshmallows in the fridge.

Mandarin Orange Marshmallows

Makes about 16 marshmallows

Marshmallow

1 portion basic gelatine-based marshmallow batter (page 20 or 28), flavoured with concentrated orange juice (page 30)

Orange gel food colouring

2 drops yellow gel food colouring

Suggested Dusting

Cornstarch or any preferred functional dusting of choice (page 37)

Suggested Filling

White chocolate and gelatine-based filling with sour citrus (yuzu) (page 48)

1 Tbsp Mandarin orange zest

Finishing

30 g finely chopped white chocolate or white chocolate chips

2 g vegetable shortening or oil

1/4–1/2 tsp matcha powder

1. Prepare baking trays with 3-cm circle template (page 132).

2. Prepare yuzu filling with mandarin orange zest mixed in. Set in 3-cm silicone hemisphere moulds. Unmould set filling and place on a lined tray. Refrigerate until ready to assemble.

3. Prepare orange marshmallow batter with a slightly stiffer consistency for piping taller mounds for oranges. Heat syrup to 118°C–120°C. Whip Italian meringue for 3 minutes or until the meringue consistently peels off the sides of the mixing bowl before adding gelatine. Beat marshmallow batter for 3-4 minutes until firm peaks form. Add yellow and orange gel food colouring to achieve desired shade.

4. Transfer batter into a large piping bag fitted with a large round tip. I used tip #808. Pipe discs about 1–1.5 cm tall. Freeze for 2 minutes.

5. Use a skewer to scratch crosshatch lines on base and domed tops of filling. Scratching the surface of the filling helps it to adhere to the marshmallow. Place a hemisphere of filling on each disc. Position piping tip about 1–1.5 cm away from top of filling. Apply constant pressure on piping bag until batter covers filling and disc. Release pressure on piping bag and give it a quick twirl. Tap down any peaks.

6. Chill trays of piped marshmallows in the fridge for 30 minutes to 2 hours or overnight in air-conditioned room. Dust and dislodge marshmallows from baking paper.

7. Press a citrus juicer into the top of marshmallows and leave for several seconds to create indent on orange. Repeat if necessary as marshmallows may bounce back to their original shape. Dust tops of marshmallows again if juicer sticks to marshmallow during indentation.

8. Use a fine zester to scuff surface of orange to give it an orange peel texture. Use a skewer to create random pores for a more natural look. Dust surface of orange if it becomes sticky again while creating orange peel texture.

9. Melt white chocolate with a little vegetable shortening or oil. Portion out about half the melted chocolate and add matcha powder to colour it earthy green. Transfer melted white chocolate and matcha white chocolate into OPP cones. Pipe green stem, followed by a small white dollop in the middle.

10. Store in airtight containers at cool room temperature for up to 3 days or in the fridge for up to 2 weeks. Store sugar-free marshmallows in the fridge.

Cute & Magical

Lunar New Year Marshmallows

Makes about 25 marshmallows

Marshmallow

1 portion basic gelatine-based marshmallow batter (page 20 or 28)

Peach, yellow and red gel food colouring

½ tsp charcoal powder and 4–8 drops black gel food colouring

Suggested Dusting

Cornstarch or any preferred functional dusting of choice (page 37)

Finishing

Peach or pink coloured lustre dust

Dried black gel food colouring

A little water

Red sugar flowers

Note: Piping this design will take time, so pipe only as many as you are comfortable doing. Any remaining batter can be set in moulds.

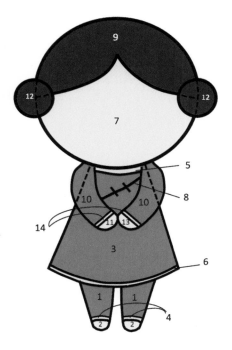

1. Prepare baking trays with Lunar New Year template (page 134).

2. Prepare marshmallow batter. Portion out 90 g and colour it peach. Portion out 70 g and colour it black. Portion out about 2 tsp and colour it yellow. Colour remaining batter red.

3. Transfer yellow batter into an OPP cone and the rest into medium piping bags. Cut a 2-mm hole at the tips. As it may take some time to pipe, place piping bags on a heating pad or in an oven with the light on.

4. Pipe girl in order and colours indicated below. Pipe layers as thickly as possible for a fluffier marshmallow character. Use a damp skewer to nudge batter into place where necessary. Freeze for 2 minutes in between piping steps as necessary to ensure adjacent portions where you want some definition remain distinct, such as the clasped hands. Reserve a little black or red marshmallow for gluing sugar flowers.

5. Leave piped marshmallows to cure overnight in an air-conditioned room.

6. Wet a superfine tip brush and dab off any excess water on a paper towel. Pick up some dried black gel food colouring and paint mouth and eyes.

7. Add rosy cheeks with peach or pink lustre dust.

8. Dust and dislodge marshmallows from baking paper.

9. Melt and stir leftover marshmallow batter and use it to glue sugar flowers on the head.

10. Store in airtight containers at cool room temperature and consume within 2 weeks. Store sugar-free marshmallows in the fridge.

Cat Marshmallows

Makes about 18 marshmallows

Marshmallow

1 portion basic gelatine-based marshmallow batter (page 20 or 28), flavoured with black tea or oolong (page 32)

2 drops chocolate paste or brown gel food colouring

Suggested Dusting

Cornstarch or any preferred functional dusting of choice (page 37)

Finishing

Red or pink heart sprinkles

Melted dark chocolate

1. Prepare baking trays with 3.5-cm circle template (page 132).

2. Prepare tea-flavoured marshmallow batter with a slightly stiffer consistency for piping taller mounds for cats. Heat syrup to 117°C–119°C. Whip Italian meringue for 3 minutes or until the meringue consistently peels off the sides of the mixing bowl before adding gelatine. Beat marshmallow batter for 3-4 minutes until firm peaks form.

3. Portion out 35 g batter and colour it dark brown. Transfer 25 g light brown batter into a small piping bag and cut a 3-mm hole at the tip. Transfer remaining light brown batter into a large piping bag fitted with a large round tip. I used tip #808. Transfer dark brown batter into small piping bag fitted with tip #7.

4. Using the large piping bag, pipe a generous mound of batter for bodies. As you release pressure on the piping bag towards the end of piping, gently bring tip upwards by about 5 mm and press down slightly while applying pressure on piping bag again to pipe heads. End off by releasing pressure on piping bag and giving it a quick flick. Tap down any peaks on the head. Freeze for 2 minutes.

5. Pipe dark brown ears. Use a damp skewer to shift batter into place as necessary.

6. Pipe dark brown tail.

7. Place a heart sprinkle over cat's chin. Pipe front paws holding heart sprinkle using light brown batter from small piping bag.

8. Refrigerate piped marshmallows for 30 minutes to 2 hours or overnight in an air-conditioned room.

9. Dust and dislodge marshmallows from baking paper.

10. Pipe the eyes and paint the nose and whiskers using melted chocolate.

11. Store in airtight containers at cool room temperature and consume within 2 weeks. Store sugar-free marshmallows in the fridge.

Narwhal Marshmallows

Makes about 18 marshmallows

Marshmallow

1 portion basic gelatine-based marshmallow batter (page 20 or 28), flavoured with mango (page 30) or passionfruit (page 31)

I drop blue gel food colouring

2 drops teal gel food colouring

Charcoal powder and/or black gel food colouring

A little warm water as needed

Suggested Dusting

Cornstarch or any preferred functional dusting of choice (page 37)

Finishing

Dried teal gel food colouring

1–2 drops white gel food colouring

1. Prepare baking trays with narwhal template (page 134).

2. Prepare marshmallow batter with a slightly stiffer consistency. Heat syrup to 118°C–120°C. Whip Italian meringue for 3 minutes or until meringue consistently peels off the sides of the mixing bowl before adding gelatine. Beat marshmallow batter for 3–4 minutes until firm peaks form.

3. Transfer 60 g batter into small piping bag fitted with tip #8. Transfer 20 g batter into a small microwaveable bowl and cover with cling wrap. Add blue and teal gel food colouring to the remaining batter to achieve a light teal colour. Transfer light teal batter into large piping bag fitted with a tip adapter and tip #10. Pipe a 5–8 mm thick layer of white batter for belly. Leave a 1–2 mm margin from template as batter will spread when body is piped. Immediately pipe body and tail using light teal batter, starting with a generous mound from body and ending with tail. Insert piping tip back into body and squeeze piping bag to add more batter to increase volume of body if needed. Tap down any peaks. Freeze for 2 minutes.

4. Switch to tip #5 for light teal. Pipe fins.

5. Soften uncoloured batter briefly in the microwave for 3 seconds at medium power and stir. Transfer into a small piping bag and cut a 2-mm hole at the tip or use tip #2. Pipe base segment of horn with uncoloured batter. Freeze for 2 minutes. Pipe middle and top segments of horn with 2 minutes of freezing between steps.

6. Transfer remaining uncoloured batter into a microwaveable bowl. Colour it black with charcoal powder and/or black gel colouring and 1–2 drops warm water. Microwave briefly if needed until batter is of a pipeable consistency. Transfer into an OPP cone and cut a small hole at the tip. Pipe eyes.

7. Leave piped marshmallows to cure overnight in an air-conditioned room.

8. Add 1–2 drops white gel colouring to moisten and lighten dried teal gel food colouring. Use a small paintbrush to create a few random spots on body. Make sure to dab the paintbrush on a paper towel to remove any excess gel before applying on marshmallow.

9. Allow painted spots to dry before dusting. To do so, leave the painted marshmallows untouched at a cool and dry place for at least 8 hours.

10. Dust and dislodge marshmallows from baking paper.

11. Store in airtight containers at cool room temperature and consume within 2 weeks. Store sugar-free marshmallows in the fridge.

Frog Prince Marshmallows

Makes about 13 marshmallows

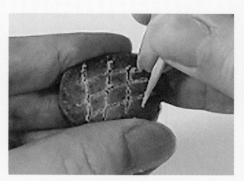

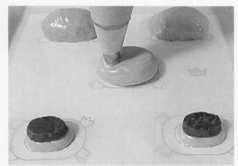

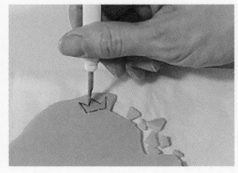

Recipe on pages 86 and 87

Marshmallow

1 portion basic gelatine-based marshmallow batter (page 20 or 28), flavoured with matcha (page 32)

Green gel food colouring

Suggested Filling

Half portion of white chocolate and gelatine-based filling with azuki bean paste (page 49)

Suggested Dusting

Cornstarch or any preferred functional dusting of choice (page 37)

1. Prepare filling and set in a 10 x 10-cm aluminium foil tray lined with baking paper. (See video.)

2. Trace smallest oblong in template (page 135) onto a clear plastic sheet. Cut out and rinse. Pat dry. Using plastic oblong, cut out 13 oblong shapes from filling with a small knife. Place on a lined tray and refrigerate until ready to assemble.

3. Prepare baking trays with frog template (page 135).

4. Prepare marshmallow batter with a slightly stiffer consistency. Heat syrup to 117°C–119°C. Whip Italian meringue for 3 minutes or until meringue consistently peels off sides of mixing bowl before adding gelatine. Beat marshmallow batter for 3–4 minutes until firm peaks form.

5. Add green colouring to get desired shade of green. You may also add colouring to syrup or matcha gelatin bloom. Transfer into a large piping bag fitted with tip #804 or cut an 8–10 mm hole at the tip. Pipe base of frog bodies by following dotted oblong outline. Freeze for 2 minutes.

6. Use a skewer to scratch crosshatch lines on surface of filling. Scratching the surface of the filling helps it to adhere to the marshmallow. Place filling on piped bases. Pipe batter to cover filling while keeping within boundary marked by largest oblong on template. Tap down any peaks. Freeze for 2 minutes.

 Scan the QR code to view a video tutorial on preparing the filling and piping frogs.

Mini chocolate chips

Peach or pink coloured lustre dust
(optional)

Yellow candy melts or white
chocolate coloured yellow

7. Transfer remaining batter into a small piping bag and cut a
2-mm hole at the tip. Pipe eyes and feet. Tap down any peaks.

8. Refrigerate piped marshmallows for 30 minutes to 2 hours or
overnight in an air-conditioned room.

9. Make yellow crown. Microwave yellow candy melts for a few
seconds at medium power and knead with a spatula or gloved
hand until it forms a ball. Repeat heating as necessary but
be careful not to melt candy melts. Roll between 2 sheets of
baking paper into a 3-mm thick sheet. Refrigerate for 5 minutes
or until firm.

10. Prepare crown template (page 135). Trace crown onto a clear
plastic sheet. Cut out and rinse. Pat dry. Using plastic crown
template, cut out 13 crown shapes from candy melt using a
small knife. Alternatively, use white chocolate coloured yellow
and pipe crowns onto lined trays. Peel off when set.

11. Attach crowns to heads. Pipe a little batter behind crowns as
support. Attach chocolate chips for eyes. Melt some chocolate
chips and paint nostrils and mouth using a skewer or small
brush. Let chocolate set completely.

12. Add rosy cheeks with peach or pink lustre dust.

13. Dust and dislodge marshmallows from baking paper.

14. Store in airtight containers at cool room temperature for up
to 3 days or in the fridge for up to 2 weeks. Store sugar-free
marshmallows in the fridge.

Teddy Bear Marshmallows

Makes about 24 marshmallows

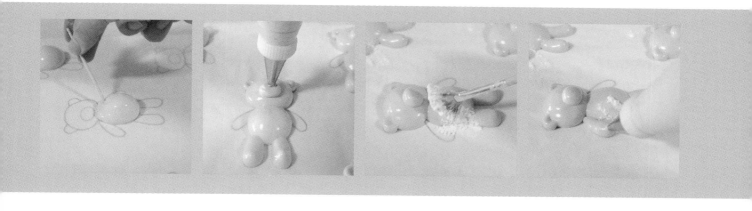

Marshmallow

1 portion basic gelatine-based marshmallow batter (page 20 or 28), flavoured with coffee (page 32)

2 cinnamon sticks (optional)

300 g water (optional)

Suggested Dusting

Cornstarch or any preferred functional dusting of choice (page 37)

Finishing

Mini chocolate crispy pearls or non pareils

1. Prepare baking trays with teddy bear template (page 135).

2. Prepare marshmallow batter. Use batter with either floppy peak or firm peak consistency depending on how full and fluffy you want the bears to be. To flavour coffee with cinnamon, boil 2 cinnamon sticks in 300 g water for 10 minutes. Remove cinnamon sticks. Chill some cinnamon water for blooming gelatine. If using brewed coffee, brew using cinnamon water.

3. Transfer batter into a large piping bag fitted with a piping tip adapter and tip #10. Pipe bodies. Begin from the neck and pipe towards the belly, piling up the batter higher at the belly. Use a skewer to nudge the batter into the neckline. Freeze for 2 minutes.

4. Pipe heads.

5. Switch to tip #6 and pipe legs, starting from body outwards.

6. Switch to tip #3 and pipe ears.

7. Switch back to tip #6 and pipe snouts.

8. Pipe arm starting from body outwards, but first pile a little dusting at the side of bear's body to prevent piped arm from sticking to the side of the body by accident, if desired.

9. Refrigerate piped marshmallows for 30 minutes to 2 hours or overnight in an air-conditioned room.

10. Use tweezers to place mini chocolate crispy pearls or non pareils for nose and eyes.

11. Dust and dislodge marshmallows from baking paper. Use a small damp brush to brush off excess dusting from the eyes and nose if necessary.

12. Store in airtight containers at cool room temperature and consume within 2 weeks. Store sugar-free marshmallows in the fridge.

Scan the QR code to view a video tutorial on piping rounded ears with a natural indent.

Unicorn Marshmallows

Makes about 16 marshmallows

Marshmallow

1 portion basic gelatine-based marshmallow batter (page 20 or 28), flavoured with osmanthus or lavender (page 32)

Pink, yellow, teal and purple gel food colouring

Charcoal powder and/or black gel food colouring

A little warm water as necessary

Suggested Dusting

Cornstarch or any preferred functional dusting of choice (page 37)

Finishing

Peach or pink coloured lustre dust

1. Prepare baking trays with unicorn templates (pages 136–137).

2. Prepare marshmallow batter with a slightly stiffer consistency. Heat syrup to 117°C–119°C. Whip Italian meringue for about 3 minutes or until meringue consistently peels off the sides of the mixing bowl before adding gelatine. Beat marshmallow batter for 3–4 minutes until firm peaks form.

3. Pipe white parts of unicorn following the sequence below. Wait for a while or freeze for 2 minutes between steps to keep parts distinct.
a) Sitting upright: (i) hind legs and body, (ii) head — pipe thinner layer of batter for snout and thicker layer for head, (iii) right foreleg, (iv) ears, (v) left foreleg.
b) Prone: (i) forelegs, followed by hind legs, then body, starting from head to rear. (ii) head — pile a little cornstarch under the chin before piping head, (iii) ears.

4. Microwave leftover marshmallow if it has stiffened up too much. Portion out about 15 g marshmallow batter into a small bowl for each colour: yellow, pink, teal and purple. Add colouring one drop at a time until desired shade is achieved. Transfer into small piping bags and cut a 2-mm hole at the tips.

5. Pipe horns, fringe, mane and tail in this sequence: (i) base segment of yellow horn, (ii) teal lock of fringe/mane/tail, (iii) middle segment of yellow horn, (iv) purple lock of fringe/mane/tail, (v) top segment of yellow horn, (vi) pink lock of fringe/mane/tail.

6. Create nostril indents by using the blunt end of a skewer or a small ball tool, dampened first with a little water.

7. Portion out 10 g leftover white batter and colour it black. Transfer into an OPP cone and pipe round eyes. Alternatively, paint round eyes using the blunt end of a skewer or a small ball tool. Use a superfine tip brush or a skewer to paint closed eyes of prone unicorns.

8. Add rosy cheeks with peach or pink lustre dust.

9. Dust and dislodge heads for sitting unicorns. Brush off excess dusting from base of heads, then brush lightly with a little water and press onto bodies.

10. Dust and dislodge marshmallows from baking paper.

11. Store in airtight containers at cool room temperature and consume within 2 weeks. Store sugar-free marshmallows in the fridge.

Shiba Inu Marshmallows

Makes about 16 marshmallows

Marshmallow

1 portion basic gelatine-based marshmallow batter (page 20 or 28), flavoured with osmanthus or lavender (page 32)

Black gel food colouring

1 drop pink gel food colouring

Charcoal powder

A little warm water as necessary

Suggested Dusting

Cornstarch or any preferred functional dusting of choice (page 37)

1. Prepare baking trays with Shiba Inu template (page 137).

2. Prepare marshmallow batter with a slightly stiffer consistency. Heat syrup to 117°C–119°C. Whip Italian meringue for 3 minutes or until meringue consistently peels off the sides of the mixing bowl before adding gelatine. Beat marshmallow batter for 3–4 minutes until firm peaks form.

3. Portion out 50 g batter into a bowl. Add warm water a few drops at a time until batter reaches a floppy peak consistency. Transfer into a medium piping bag and cut a 3-mm hole at the tip. Add black gel colouring to remaining batter until desired shade of grey. Transfer 40 g grey batter into a small piping bag and cut a 3-mm hole at the tip. Transfer remaining grey batter into a large piping bag fitted with a large round tip. (I used tip #807.)

4. Pipe body using grey batter from large piping bag, followed by a white belly. Smoothen out any peaks with a damp skewer. Freeze for 2 minutes.

5. Pipe front legs, starting with white paws and followed by grey part of forelegs using grey batter from small piping bag. Smoothen out boundary between different coloured batters on each leg with a damp skewer. Freeze for 2 minutes.

6. Pipe hind legs, starting with grey part of leg at rump and followed by white paws.

7. Pipe a round mound for head using grey batter from large piping bag. Stick tip of small piping bag with grey batter into head where cheeks are and pipe a little batter to create puffy cheeks. Immediately pipe white face patches. Use a damp skewer to nudge batter into place as needed and smoothen out any peaks. Repeat to pipe heads, cheeks and patches. Pipe the eyebrows. Freeze for 2 minutes.

8. Pipe tails and ears using grey batter from small bag. Pipe inner ears and snouts using white batter. Freeze for 5 minutes.

9. In the meantime, portion out 1½–2 tsp white batter and colour it pink. Transfer into an OPP cone and cut a 1-mm hole at the tip. Portion out about 1 Tbsp white batter and colour it black using charcoal powder and/or black gel colouring. Transfer part or all of it into an OPP cone and cut a 1-mm hole at the tip.

10. Pipe noses. Pipe eyes or paint with a superfine brush or skewer. Pipe rosy cheeks. Optional: Pipe or paint mouths and tongues.

11. Refrigerate piped marshmallows for 30 minutes to 2 hours or overnight in an air-conditioned room.

12. Dust and dislodge marshmallows from baking paper.

13. Store in airtight containers at cool room temperature and consume within 2 weeks. Store sugar-free marshmallows in the fridge.

Penguin Marshmallows

Makes about 15 marshmallows

Recipe on pages 96 and 97

Marshmallow

1 portion basic gelatine-based marshmallow batter (page 20 or 28)

2 drops yellow gel food colouring

1 small drop orange gel food colouring

½ tsp ube or purple yam paste/extract

3 drops blue gel food colouring

2 drops of purple gel food colouring

A little warm water as necessary

1. Prepare baking trays with penguin body template (page 138) and penguin flipper template (page 138).

2. Prepare marshmallow batter but with a slightly stiffer consistency for piping taller mounds for bodies. Add ube or purple yam extract to the syrup and heat syrup to 118°C–120°C. Whip Italian meringue for 3 minutes or until the meringue consistently peels off the sides of the mixing bowl before adding gelatine. Beat marshmallow batter for 3 minutes until firm peaks form.

3. Portion out 30 g batter into a bowl. Add warm water a few drops at a time until batter reaches a floppy peak consistency. Transfer into a medium piping bag and cut a 3-mm hole at the tip.

4. Portion out 10 g batter into small microwaveable bowl and colour it dark yellow. Cover with cling wrap and set aside.

5. Add blue and purple colouring to remaining batter. Transfer purplish-blue batter into a large piping bag fitted with a large round tip (#806 or #807).

6. Pipe a tall mound that tapers slightly at the top for body using purplish-blue batter from large piping bag. Tap down any peaks. Immediately pipe face and belly patch using white batter. Tap down any peaks. Repeat to pipe bodies. Refrigerate while working on flippers.

7. Transfer leftover purplish-blue batter into a microwaveable bowl, add a little warm water and microwave as necessary to achieve floppy peak consistency. Transfer into a medium piping bag and cut a 4–5-mm hole at the tip. Pipe flippers and tap down any peaks.

8. Transfer yellow batter into a small piping bag and cut a 2-mm hole at the tip. Pipe beaks and feet. Pipe the first and third toes of the feet. Freeze for 2 minutes before piping the middle toe. This helps to create a clear definition between the toes.

9. Refrigerate piped marshmallows for 30 minutes to 2 hours or overnight in an air-conditioned room.

Cornstarch or any preferred
  functional dusting of choice
  (page 37)

Finishing

Melted dark chocolate

Melted white chocolate

Peach or pink coloured lustre dust

10. Dust and dislodge flippers from baking paper.

11. Pile a little dusting at side of bodies where flippers are to
    go. Cut end of flippers with scissors to make them shorter
    if necessary. Make a diagonal cut such that the bottom
    surface of the flipper is shorter than the upper surface.
    This increases the surface area for attaching the flipper to
    the body. Brush body of penguin with a little water. Attach
    flippers to bodies.

12. Dust assembled marshmallows and dislodge using an
    acetate sheet.

13. Paint or pipe eyes using melted dark chocolate, followed
    by white highlights with melted white chocolate. Add rosy
    cheeks with peach or pink lustre dust.

14. Store in airtight containers at cool room temperature and
    consume within 2 weeks. Store sugar-free marshmallows
    in the fridge.

Gingerbread Man Marshmallows

Makes about 24 marshmallows

Marshmallow

1 portion basic gelatine-based
  marshmallow batter (page 20),
  flavoured with gingerbread spice
  (page 32)

Suggested Dusting

Cornstarch or any preferred
  functional dusting of choice
  mixed with gingerbread spice
  (pages 37–38)

Finishing

Melted white chocolate

Melted dark chocolate

Pink powder or oil-based food
  colouring

Black cocoa powder, charcoal
  powder or black oil-based
  food colouring

Different colours of round sprinkles

1. Prepare baking trays with gingerbread man template (page 139).

2. Prepare marshmallow batter. Transfer into a large piping bag
   fitted with a #8 piping tip.

3. Pipe gingerbread men starting from limbs and piping towards
   body. Pipe body beginning with belly, then moving tip of piping
   bag towards neck. Lastly, pipe head. Tap down any peaks.

4. Refrigerate piped marshmallows for 30 minutes to 2 hours or
   overnight in an air-conditioned room.

5. Attach 2 round sprinkles for the buttons.

6. Sift together 1 part gingerbread spice to 12 parts functional
   dusting of choice. Dust and dislodge marshmallows from baking
   paper.

7. Transfer some melted white chocolate into an OPP cone. Cut
   a small hole at the tip and pipe zigzag lines on heads, arms
   and legs. Colour some melted dark chocolate black and some
   melted white chocolate pink. Transfer both into OPP cones and
   cut a small hole at the tips. Pipe eyes, mouths and rosy cheeks.
   Let chocolate set completely.

8. Store in airtight containers at cool room temperature and
   consume within 2 weeks. Note that there is no sugar-free
   variation for this due to the use of brown sugar and dark corn
   syrup as part of the flavouring.

Variation

Instead of piping, the marshmallows can also be cut out using
gingerbread man cookie cutters. For this method, prepare marshmallow
batter with a runnier consistency by bringing syrup temperature to
110°C–113°C and whipping marshmallow batter for 3–4 minutes.
Pour batter into a tray lined with greased baking paper. Make sure
the batter height does not exceed 15 mm for a cleaner cut. Oil cookie
cutter before using. Dust cut sides and toss in a sieve to remove
excess dusting. Decorate as desired.

Duckling Marshmallows

Makes about 20 marshmallows

Recipe on pages 102 and 103

Marshmallow

1 portion basic gelatine-based
marshmallow batter (page 20),
flavoured with passionfruit honey
(page 31)

Yellow gel food colouring

1 drop orange gel food colouring

A little warm water as necessary

1. Prepare fine yellow desiccated coconut for coating duckling. This can be done ahead and stored in airtight container at room temperature. Stir some yellow gel food colouring into 60 g water. Add coloured water 1 tsp at a time to desiccated coconut, mixing well until desired shade is achieved. Place yellow desiccated coconut in a 100°C-oven for 1–2 hours to dry. Grind and sift for a finer and more even coating.

2. Prepare baking trays with duckling template (page 139).

3. Prepare marshmallow batter with a slightly stiffer consistency. Use honey as the inverted sugar. Heat syrup to 118°C–120°C. Whip Italian meringue for 3 minutes or until the meringue consistently peels off the sides of the mixing bowl before adding gelatine. Beat marshmallow batter for 3–4 minutes until firm peaks form.

4. Add yellow gel food colouring to batter until shade of yellow matches yellow desiccated coconut. Portion out 15 g batter into a small microwaveable bowl and cover with cling wrap. Transfer 30 g batter into a small piping bag and cut a 3-mm hole at the tip. Keep this piping bag in the oven with the light on. Transfer remaining yellow batter into a large piping bag fitted with a large round tip (#807).

5. Pipe bodies using batter from large piping bag, starting from front end and gradually releasing pressure on the piping bag as you reach the rear end. Jerk piping bag upwards and away from the body to end off. Freeze for 2 minutes.

6. Pipe generous round mounds for heads using the same piping bag. Release pressure on piping bag before lifting off. Tap down any peaks.

7. Pipe wings using small piping bag. Tap down any peaks.

Cornstarch or any preferred
functional dusting of choice
(page 37)

90 g desiccated coconut

Yellow gel food colouring

60 g water

Finishing

Mini black chocolate chips or
melted dark chocolate coloured
black with black cocoa powder,
charcoal powder or black oil-
based colouring

Melted white chocolate (optional)

8. Freeze piped marshmallows for 15 minutes.

9. Coat marshmallows with yellow desiccated coconut and brush
off excess. Do not dislodge marshmallows from baking paper yet.

10. Soften reserved batter by microwaving for 3 seconds and
stirring. Repeat if necessary until pipeable but not too runny.
Colour it orange and transfer into a small piping bag. Cut a
2–3-mm hole at the tip. Pipe beaks.

11. Add eyes by gluing on mini black chocolate chips with a
little batter or piping using black melted dark chocolate in an
OPP cone. Add white highlights in eyes if desired using melted
white chocolate.

12. Refrigerate piped marshmallows for 30 minutes to 2 hours
or overnight in an air-conditioned room.

13. Use a small brush to dust beaks with functional dusting.

14. Dislodge marshmallows from baking paper using an acetate
sheet to push yellow desiccated coconut under marshmallows.

15. Store in airtight containers at cool room temperature and
consume within 2 weeks. Note that there is no sugar-free
variation of this marshmallow unless honey is not used as part of
the flavouring.

Perfectly Matched

Succulents-in-Pots Marshmallows

Makes 25–35 marshmallows

Recipe on pages 108 and 109

Marshmallow

1 portion basic agar-based marshmallow batter (page 24 or page 29), flavoured with matcha (page 34)

1 portion basic agar-based marshmallow batter (page 24 or page 29), flavoured with raspberry (page 33)

Various shades of green gel food colouring (avocado, leaf green, forest green etc.)

Black gel food colouring

Soft pink and dusty pink gel food colouring

1 tsp matcha powder (for raspberry batter)

Suggested Filling

Chocolate and hazelnut confection (for round cacti)

Suggested Dusting

Icing sugar, cornstarch or any preferred functional dusting of choice (page 37)

Finishing

Melted white chocolate

Red and orange oil-based food colouring

Toasted chopped hazelnuts or almonds

Dark chocolate ganache (page 44)

Store-bought or homemade tart shells

Scan the QR code to view a video tutorial on piping succulents.

1. Prepare baking paper squares or lined baking trays according to type of succulent. Prepare piping bags with appropriate piping tips for each type of succulent.

2. Divide matcha marshmallow batter into 2 equal portions. Colour one portion light green and the other dark green. Add black gel food colouring to deepen dark green if desired. Transfer into respective piping bags for succulent of choice. Complete piping first batch (matcha) before making second batch (raspberry) of batter.

3. Leave piped marshmallows out to dry overnight or for at least 8 hours. Dust and peel succulents off baking paper.

4. Transfer melted white chocolate into an OPP cone and pipe thorns on dark green cacti. Colour some white chocolate vermilion using red and orange colouring. Wait for coloured chocolate to stiffen slightly so it can hold a firm peak. Transfer to small piping bag and cut a 1-mm hole at the tip. Create blooms on dark green cacti by piping several short strips of vermilion chocolate.

5. Prepare dark chocolate ganache. Fill tart shells with ganache and set in the fridge. Arrange succulents on ganache. Cover exposed ganache with chopped toasted nuts of choice. Store in the fridge and consume within 3 days. Alternatively, store marshmallows in airtight containers at cool room temperature and arrange when ready to serve.

Simple Cacti with Blooms

Piping tip: Any large open star tip (e.g. #869 or #868) with numerous tines for main cactus body. Smaller open star tip (e.g. #862) for arms. Use separate piping bags or use tip adapters for changing tips.

Batter: Light green

Method: Prepare lined trays. Pipe tall mounds using large piping tip, keeping them 8 cm apart. Pipe arms with small piping tip. Pipe mini cacti with small tip. Pipe pink blooms using raspberry batter. Tap down any peaks with a damp finger.

Round Cacti with Thorns and Blooms

Piping tip: Tip #104

Batter: Dark green

Method: Prepare 8-cm baking paper squares. Draw a 4-cm circle on each square. Stick a paper square, circle-side down on a flower nail using a little batter. Pipe a mound of batter about 1–1.5-cm high and 4-cm wide. Place chocolate confection on top. Cover chocolate by piping batter vertically from base up and rotating flower nail.

Simple Cacti with Blooms

Round Cacti with Thorns and Blooms

Green Rose

Aloe Vera

Two-toned Desert Rose

Pipe vertical spines of cactus. Place piping tip at the top of batter-coated chocolate with narrow end of tip facing upwards and broad end touching marshmallow. Apply constant pressure on piping bag while bringing piping tip down the side of marshmallow. End off by releasing pressure on bag when tip reaches base of marshmallow. Repeat. Add blooms and thorns using melted chocolate.

Green Rose

Piping tip: Tip #104 or #125 depending on preferred size

Batter: Dark green or light green

Method: Prepare 6-cm baking paper squares. Stick a square of paper on a flower nail using a little batter. Follow piping steps for roses (page 56). Portion out 140 g raspberry marshmallow batter and colour it pink. Add 1 tsp matcha powder to remaining portion and mix well. Add some green colouring to achieve a pale earthy shade of green. Portion out 25 g pink batter and colour it dark pink. Transfer into a small piping bag fitted with a small open star tip of choice. I used tip #21. Pipe small dollops of batter for blooms on top of some cacti or on lined tray.

Aloe Vera

Piping tip: Large leaf tip (e.g. #366) resembling open beak of bird

Batter: Fill one side of piping bag with light pink batter and the other with light earthy green batter.

Method: Test and pipe a little batter from bag. Ensure both colours come out together before starting. Prepare 6-cm and/or 8-cm baking paper squares according to desired size of aloe vera. Stick a paper square on a flower nail using a little batter. Place leaf tip with lower beak of tip against flower nail and tip angled at 45° to baking paper. Apply pressure to piping bag and pull away from surface of paper as you release pressure. Pipe a ring of leaves. Pipe another ring of leaves within first ring. Repeat until there is no space to add more leaves in the middle.

Two-toned Desert Rose

Piping tip: Curved petal tip (e.g. #121 or #122)

Batter: Fill one side of piping bag with light pink batter and the other with light earthy green batter.

Method: Test and pipe a little batter from bag. Ensure both colours come out together before starting. Prepare 6-cm baking paper squares. Stick a paper square on a flower nail using a little batter. Pipe a 2–3-cm mound of batter. Pipe a strip of batter across mound such that it forms an X. Pipe rose petals following piping steps for roses (page 56).

109

Polar Bear S'mores

Makes 48 marshmallows

Recipe on pages 112 and 113

Marshmallow

1 portion basic gelatine-based marshmallow batter (page 20 or 28)

Charcoal powder and/or black gel food colouring

Pink and/or red gel food colouring

A little warm water as necessary

Suggested Dusting

Cornstarch or any preferred functional dusting of choice (page 37), optional if piping marshmallows directly on crackers

1. Polar bears can be piped freehand directly on prepared crackers or using the template. Make crackers ahead if piping freehand.

2. If using template, prepare baking trays with polar bear template (page 140).

3. Prepare marshmallow batter. Portion out 20 g batter into a small bowl and colour it dark pink or red. Transfer into a small piping bag and cut a 1–2-mm hole at the tip. Transfer 40 g batter into small piping bag and cut a 2–3-mm hole at the tip. Transfer the rest of the batter into a large piping bag and cut a 8-mm hole at the tip. Pipe polar bear heads, followed by bodies using large piping bag. Let batter pile up a little higher for heads and bellies. Tap down any peaks.

4. Pipe little hearts on bellies with dark pink or red batter. Use a skewer to adjust shape as necessary or to flatten any peaks. Freeze for 2 minutes.

5. Pipe muzzles, arms, legs and ears using white batter from small piping bag.

6. Transfer about 10 g white batter into a small bowl and colour it black. Transfer into an OPP cone and cut as small a hole as possible. Pipe noses and eyes.

7. If the template was used, refrigerate piped marshmallows for 30 minutes to 2 hours or overnight in an air-conditioned room. Dust and dislodge marshmallows from baking paper.

8. If marshmallows were piped directly on crackers, no dusting is necessary. Chill in the fridge for 30 minutes.

9. Store marshmallows/marshmallows on crackers in airtight containers at cool room temperature for 2–4 days to dry them out. Store sugar-free marshmallows in the fridge. This step of drying is necessary if toasting the marshmallows as homemade marshmallows contain more moisture than store-bought ones. Drying also helps the marshmallows retain their shape.

Graham Crackers

400 g wholemeal flour

240 g light brown sugar

1–2 tsp ground cinnamon

1½ tsp baking soda

1 tsp salt

140 g unsalted butter, cut into
  cubes, softened but still firm

70 g milk

110 g honey

4 tsp vanilla extract

Chocolate Layer

175 g dark chocolate, finely
  chopped

35 g butter

10. Prepare Graham cracker dough. Whisk together flour, sugar, salt, cinnamon and baking soda in a mixing bowl. Add butter and use fingertips to rub in until mixture resembles fine breadcrumbs.

11. In a measuring jug, mix together honey, milk and vanilla. Pour into flour mixture and mix to form a dough. The dough will be sticky.

12. Divide dough into 2 portions and roll each one between baking paper into a 6-mm thick sheet. Freeze overnight or for at least 1 hour until firm.

13. Preheat oven to 175°C/160°C (fan). Line baking trays with a perforated mat or baking paper.

14. Cut cookie dough using a 4.5 x 5.5-cm cookie cutter or use a ruler and knife/pizza cutter to cut out rectangles. Place cut-outs at least 2 cm apart. Bake for 9–11 minutes. The crackers will be soft when hot and will harden when cool. Adjust baking temperature and time according to your oven.

15. Prepare chocolate layer. Melt chocolate and butter until smooth using double-boiling method or microwave oven. Transfer into a piping bag and cut a small hole at the tip. Pipe chocolate on cooled crackers. Let set in an air-conditioned room for 30 minutes or in the fridge for 10 minutes. Store in airtight containers in single layers separated by baking paper until ready to pipe/toast with marshmallows.

16. To toast, place assembled crackers on a baking tray. Use toaster oven or broiler function of oven and toast for 1–3 minutes, checking every 10 seconds after the first 30 seconds. Place marshmallows about 5 cm away from top heating element and as far away as possible from bottom heating element. Be careful not to let it burn it as it can turn from white to charred within 20–30 seconds.

17. Consume freshly toasted.

Koalas on Biscuit Sticks

Makes 35–40 marshmallows

Recipe on pages 116 and 117

Marshmallow

1 portion basic gelatine-based marshmallow batter (page 20 or 28), flavoured with green tea infusion (page 32)

2 drops chocolate paste or 1 small drop brown gel food colouring

Black gel food colouring

A little warm water as necessary

Charcoal powder

Suggested Dusting

Cornstarch or any preferred functional dusting of choice (page 37)

Finishing

Melted white chocolate

Matcha powder

Melted milk chocolate

35–40 biscuit sticks, each 8–10-mm thick and 10–12-cm long

Note: 35–40 koalas is a lot to pipe, so make only as many marshmallows as you are comfortable with. Any extra marshmallow batter can be set in a greased mould or tray and cut into cubes for serving.

1. Prepare baking trays with leaf template (page 141). Place some melted white chocolate in a small bowl. Add matcha powder to colour it to your desired shade of green. Transfer into an OPP cone or small piping bag and pipe leaves. Set in the fridge for about 5 minutes or in an air-conditioned room until firm. Remove leaves and set aside.

2. Place some melted milk chocolate in a small deep bowl or mug. Dip biscuit sticks into chocolate until only about 1-1.5 cm is left uncoated. Shake off excess chocolate and lay coated biscuits on lined trays. Attach matcha white chocolate leaves before dark chocolate sets. Use koala template (page 140) as reference for where to position leaves if needed. Bear in mind to leave sufficient space for piping marshmallows. Set in the fridge for about 5 minutes or in an air-conditioned room until firm. Using a knife, score chocolate coating on biscuit to create texture of "branch" or "trunk" if desired.

3. Store in airtight containers while making marshmallows.

4. Prepare baking trays with koala template (page 140).

5. Prepare marshmallow batter. Transfer about 40 g batter into a bowl and add a few drops of warm water to thin out batter slightly. Transfer into a small piping bag and cut a 2-mm hole at the tip. Add chocolate paste or brown gel food colouring, and black gel colouring to rest of batter until desired shade of warm grey is achieved. Transfer about 40 g batter into a small piping bag and cut a 2-mm hole at the tip. Transfer rest of grey batter into a large piping bag and cut a 4-mm hole at the tip.

6. Arrange biscuit sticks on prepared trays following template except for koala hanging vertically. Pipe body using batter from large piping bag for all 3 designs. Immediately pipe white belly for hanging and sleeping koalas. Tap down any peaks. Freeze for 2 minutes.

7. Pipe heads using batter from large piping bag. Pipe hind legs with grey batter from small piping bag. Freeze for 2 minutes.

8. Pipe outer and inner ears using batter from small piping bags. Pipe arms with grey batter from small piping bag on upright and lying koalas. Place biscuit stick on koala that is hanging vertically. Use a small sheet of paper towel to prop one end of biscuit stick to keep it horizontal if needed. Pipe arms on hanging koala. Tap down any peaks.

9. Transfer about 15 g leftover grey batter into a small microwaveable bowl. Add some charcoal powder and/or black gel food colouring. Microwave for 3 seconds and stir until it is a pipeable consistency. Add a little warm water if necessary. Pipe or paint eyes and noses.

10. Refrigerate piped marshmallows for 30 minutes to 2 hours or overnight in an air-conditioned room.

11. Dust and dislodge marshmallows from baking paper. Avoid applying too much dusting on chocolate-coated biscuit.

12. Store in airtight containers at cool room temperature and consume within 2 weeks.

Brown Sugar Dorayaki Sloths

Makes 25–25 marshmallows

Recipe on pages 120 and 121

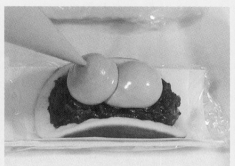

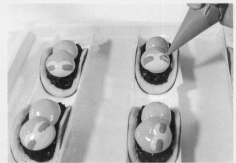

Marshmallow

1 portion basic gelatine-based marshmallow batter (page 20 or 28), flavoured with brown sugar caramel (page 31)

White gel food colouring

1 drop black gel food colouring

1–2 drops chocolate paste or 1 drop brown gel food colouring

A little warm water as necessary

Note: Store-bought azuki bean paste is convenient, but they tend to be very sweet. If you prefer something less sweet, make your own from using the recipe for azuki bean paste (page 49). Adjust with salt and sugar to taste (or 25%–50% weight of red bean purée) and cook over medium-low heat until sugar is dissolved. Add a little water as necessary while cooking. Set aside to cool completely uncovered before using. Azuki bean paste will keep indefinitely stored in the freezer.

1. Prepare pancakes. Take paper kitchen towel cardboard tubes and cut into half lengthwise to create holders for pancakes. Wrap with cling wrap or aluminium foil. Place each pancake on a square of parchment paper, then gently fit 2 pancakes into each cardboard tube holder. Fill pancakes with azuki bean paste. Smoothen top surface of filling. Store in airtight containers.

2. Prepare marshmallow batter. Portion out 30 g batter and add white gel colouring to achieve a lighter shade of brown. Add 1–2 drops warm water to thin batter if necessary so face patches will appear smooth. Transfer into a small piping bag and cut a 2-mm hole at the tip.

3. Add a drop of black gel food colouring to the rest of brown batter to achieve a greyish hue.

4. Transfer 20 g greyish brown batter into a small bowl and add chocolate paste or brown gel food colouring to colour it dark brown. Add 1–2 drops warm water to thin it a little so eye patches will appear smooth. Transfer into a small piping bag and cut a 1–2-mm hole at the tip.

5. Transfer rest of brown batter into large piping bag and cut a 4-mm hole at the tip.

Suggested Dusting

Cornstarch or any preferred
functional dusting of choice
(page 37), optional if piping
marshmallows directly on
dorayaki

Finishing

20–25 pancakes, each 8–10 cm
in diameter, made using pancake
mix of choice

Azuki bean paste (*see* Note)

Melted white chocolate

Melted dark chocolate

Charcoal powder, black cocoa
powder or black oil-based
food colouring (optional)

6. Sloths can be piped freehand directly on prepared pancakes
    or using the template (page 141) on baking trays.

7. Pipe bodies using brown batter from large piping bag. Start
    from neck and pile up more batter towards the backside. Tap
    down any peaks. Freeze for 2 minutes.

8. Pipe heads using brown batter from large piping bag, followed
    immediately by face patches using light brown batter, and eye
    patches using dark brown batter.

9. Pipe arms and legs using brown batter from small piping bag.

10. Melt white chocolate and transfer into an OPP cone. Cut a
    small hole at the tip and pipe claws.

11. If the template was used, refrigerate piped marshmallows for
    30 minutes to 2 hours or overnight in an air-conditioned room.
    Dust and dislodge marshmallows from baking paper.

12. If marshmallows were piped directly on pancakes, no dusting
    is necessary. Chill in the fridge for 30 minutes.

13. Pipe or paint eyes, noses and mouths using melted dark
    chocolate. Colour chocolate black, if desired, using charcoal
    powder, black cocoa powder or black oil-based food colouring.

14. Serve immediately. If making ahead of time, store in airtight
    containers at cool room temperature and consume within
    2 days. These *dorayaki* will keep in the fridge for up to
    7 days or in the freezer for up to a few weeks. Bear in mind
    that marshmallows and *dorayaki* will become drier with storage.

Strawberry Hedgehog Pastries

Makes about 10 pastries

Recipe on pages 124 and 125

Marshmallow

1 portion basic gelatine-based
  marshmallow batter (page 20
  or 28)

¼ tsp chocolate paste or
  brown gel food colouring

Puff Pastry

Frozen puff pastry sheets, enough
  for making 10 rectangles, each
  14 x 7 cm, thawed

1 egg, lightly beaten

2 tsp water

Mascarpone Whipped Cream

150 g freshly whipped cream (dairy
  or non-dairy)

120 g mascarpone cheese

1 tsp vanilla bean paste or extract

30 g icing sugar (optional if using
  sweetened non-dairy whipped
  cream)

Finishing

30 strawberries, preferably with
  pointed ends

Store-bought or homemade glaze
  for pastries (optional)

300 g dark chocolate ganache
  (page 44)

Black cocoa powder, charcoal
  powder or black oil-based
  food colouring

1. Preheat oven to 200°C.

2. Make pastry base. Cut puff pastry sheets into 14 x 7-cm rectangles. Arrange at least 2 cm apart on a baking tray lined with a perforated mat (preferable) or baking paper. Use a knife to score a border around each sheet, about 1.5 cm from edge. Be careful to cut only the top few layers of pastry and not all the way through. Use a fork to pierce surface of pastry within the smaller rectangle to allow pastry to puff up more along the borders and remain flatter in the middle.

3. In a small bowl, whisk together egg and water. Brush border of pastry with egg wash.

4. Bake for 15–20 minutes or until golden brown. Using the back of a spoon, immediately press down centre of pastry, leaving border raised. Set aside to cool.

5. While pastry is baking, prepare dark chocolate ganache using a chocolate to cream ratio that is able to hold a stiff peak when set at your ambient temperature. Set aside at cool room temperature to firm up while preparing mascarpone whipped cream. If using dairy cream, whip chilled cream with icing sugar and vanilla until firm peaks form. Be careful not to overwhip. If using non-dairy whipping cream, whip vanilla together with chilled cream until stiff peaks form.

6. In a separate bowl, whisk mascarpone briefly. Fold whipped cream into mascarpone until well combined. Cover and refrigerate until ready to assemble.

7. Prepare strawberries. Hull strawberries, then cut pointed ends off strawberries for the caps. Caps should be about one-quarter the length of strawberries. Place strawberries, both caps and bottoms, cut side down on a tray lined with paper towels. Refrigerate until ready to assemble.

8. Spoon 220 g mascarpone whipped cream into a large piping bag and cut a 8–10-mm hole at the tip. Keep remaining cream covered in the fridge. Pipe a layer of cream on cooled pastry and smoothen out surface with a spatula.

9. Place 3 strawberries on piped cream with larger cut surface of bottom piece facing up. Glaze strawberries if desired.

10. Transfer some chocolate ganache into a piping bag and coat exposed cut surface of strawberries. This is to insulate the marshmallow from the wet surface of the strawberry. Store in fridge while preparing marshmallow batter.

11. Prepare marshmallow batter but with a stiffer consistency. Add yellow gel colouring and chocolate paste or brown gel colouring to syrup. Heat syrup to 117°C–119°C. Whip Italian meringue for 3 minutes or until meringue consistently peels off sides of mixing bowl before adding gelatine. Beat marshmallow batter for 3–4 minutes until firm peaks form.

12. Transfer 50 g batter into small piping bag and cut a 2-mm hole at the tip. Transfer rest of batter into a large piping bag and cut a 5–6-mm hole cut.

13. Pipe a generous mound of batter on chocolate-coated surface of strawberries for head of hedgehogs using batter from large piping bag. Tap down any peaks. Freeze for 2 minutes.

14. Pipe snouts, hands and ears using batter from small piping bag.

15. Cover area with quills using dark chocolate ganache. The ganache does not have to be applied smoothly. Dip a skewer into ganache and quickly lift off surface to create dark chocolate ganache quills. If ganache is too soft to hold peaks, freeze for 1–2 minutes before attempting again.

16. Colour leftover ganache black using black cocoa powder, charcoal powder or black oil-based colouring. Heat ganache in microwave oven and stir until smooth and runny. Pipe or paint facial features.

17. Transfer remaining mascarpone whipped cream into a small piping bag and cut a 1–2-mm hole at the tip. Attach strawberry caps to hedgehog with a little cream. Glaze strawberry caps if desired. Pipe dollops of mascarpone cream around base and top of strawberry caps.

18. Place pastry on individual cake boards or serving plates. Keep refrigerated until ready to serve. Consume within 2 days.

Lions and Tigers Orange-Chocolate Hazelnut Spread Toast

Makes 10 pieces

Marshmallow

1 portion basic gelatine-based
  marshmallow batter (page 20
  or 28), flavoured with orange
  (page 30)

Orange gel food colouring

3–4 drops chocolate paste

Charcoal powder and/or
  black gel food colouring

A little warm water as necessary

Finishing

10 slices sandwich bread

Chocolate hazelnut spread

1. Spread bread with a thin layer of chocolate hazelnut spread.

2. Prepare marshmallow batter. Portion 20 g batter into a small piping bag and cut a 2-mm hole at the tip. Divide rest of batter into 2 equal portions. Colour one portion orange. Transfer 20 g orange batter into a small piping bag and cut a 2-mm hole at the tip. Transfer the rest into a large piping bag and cut a 8–10-mm hole at the tip. Colour other portion light brown using chocolate paste. Transfer 20 g light brown batter into a small piping bag and cut a 2-mm hole at the tip. Transfer the rest into a large piping bag and cut a 8–10-mm hole at the tip.

3. Create base of tiger head by piping an oblong-shaped dollop of orange batter on top left corner of toast. Use the back of a clean metal spoon to flatten and smoothen out batter. Repeat with light brown batter for lion head. Create a 3 x 4 grid, alternating tiger and lion heads.

4. Pipe tiger ears with orange batter and lion ears with brown batter from small piping bags. Use a skewer to nudge batter into place if necessary. Pipe inner ears and muzzles using uncoloured batter.

5. Colour a little leftover batter black using charcoal powder and/or black gel food colouring. Microwave batter and add a drop of warm water if necessary. Transfer into an OPP cone and cut a small hole at the tip. Pipe facial features and tiger stripes.

6. Transfer some chocolate hazelnut spread into a small piping bag and cut a 2-mm hole at the tip. Pipe lion manes, letting chocolate hazelnut spread fall from piping bag like a strand of noodle.

7. Store in airtight containers until ready to serve. Consume within 2 days.

Healthy Octopus Parfait

Makes 20 parfaits

Marshmallow

1 portion basic gelatine-based marshmallow batter (page 20 or 28), flavoured with lemon or lime (page 30)

Blue and teal gel food colouring

Suggested Dusting

Cornstarch or any preferred functional dusting of choice (page 37), optional if piping marshmallows directly on parfait

Finishing

Melted dark chocolate

Melted white chocolate

Pink oil-based colouring

Parfait

Fresh mango slices cut into star shapes using star cookie cutter

Mango Greek yoghurt or yoghurt of choice

Granola and/or chopped toasted nuts of choice

1. Octopuses can be piped freehand directly on prepared parfait or using template (page 142) on baking trays. Make marshmallows ahead if using template.

2. Prepare parfait. Pipe some yoghurt into 20 serving glasses. Line wall of glasses with star-shaped mango slices. Add more yoghurt to cover mango. Fill middle of glasses with mango, granola and/or chopped toasted nuts. Cover top of yoghurt with granola and/or chopped toasted nuts. Refrigerate until ready to serve or pipe marshmallows.

3. Prepare marshmallow batter. Divide batter into 2 equal portions. Colour one portion teal and the other blue. Transfer batter into large piping bags fitted with tip #8.

4. Pipe octopus tentacles starting from end of tentacle towards centre. Freeze for 2 minutes. Pipe generous mounds of batter for heads. Tap down any peaks.

5. If using template, refrigerate piped marshmallows for 30 minutes to 2 hours or overnight in an air-conditioned room. Dust and dislodge marshmallows from baking paper.

6. If piping directly on parfait, chill in the fridge for 30 minutes.

7. Pipe or paint facial features using melted dark chocolate and white chocolate coloured pink.

8. Keep refrigerated until ready to serve. Consume within a day.

Design Templates

Use these templates to guide you in piping the marshmallow batter as well as some chocolate deco parts. Make a photocopy of your chosen design and enlarge it by 200%. Arrange the template on the baking tray, place a sheet of baking paper over it and grease before piping. The template can be kept and reused each time you bake.

4-cm Circles
(Enlarge 200%)

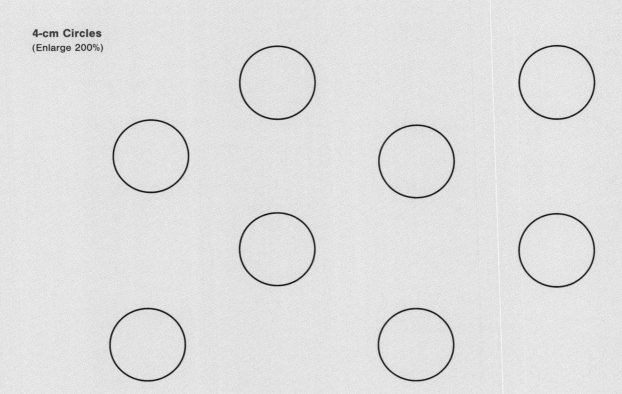

4.5-cm Circles
(Enlarge 200%)

5-cm Circles
(Enlarge 200%)

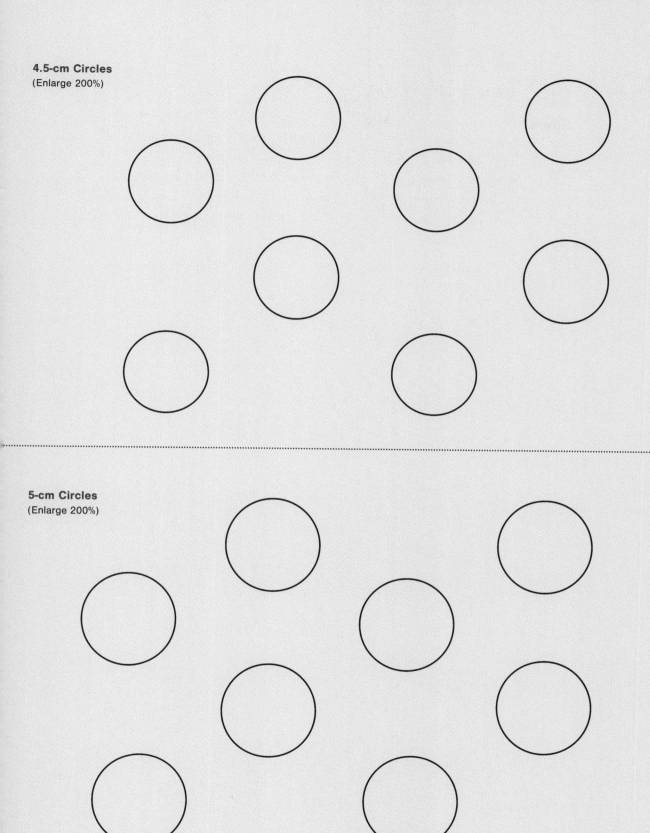

3-cm Circles
(Enlarge 200%)

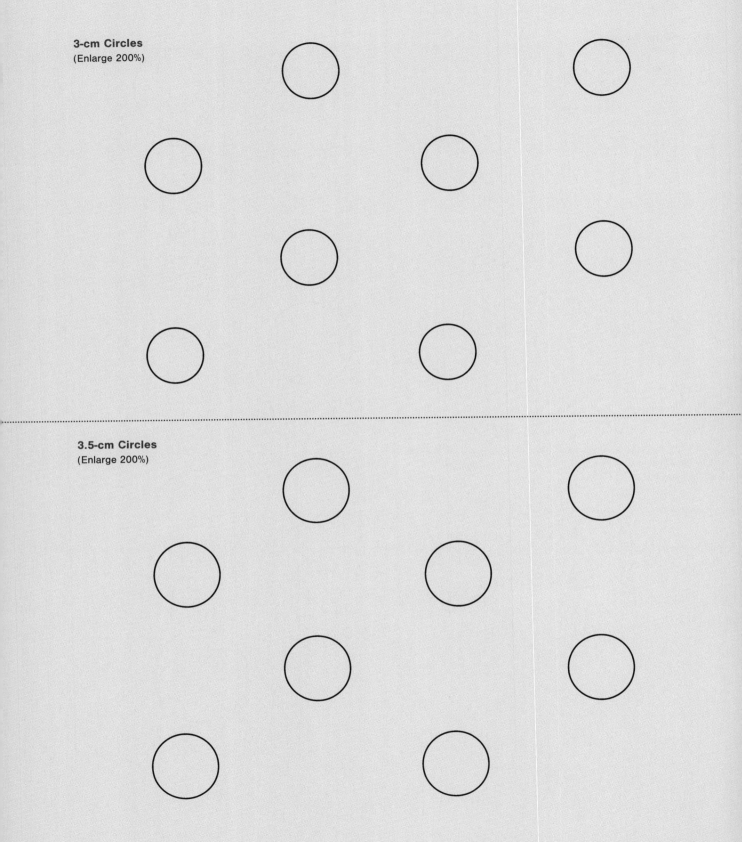

3.5-cm Circles
(Enlarge 200%)

Rainbow (page 70)
(Enlarge 200%)

Cloud (page 70)
(Enlarge 200%)

Lunar New Year (page 78)
(Enlarge 200%)

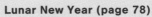

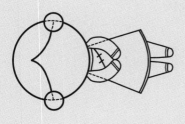
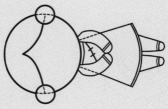

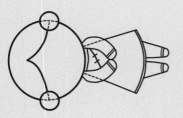
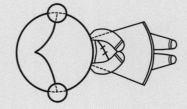

Narwhal (page 82)
(Enlarge 200%)

Frog Prince (page 84)
(Enlarge 200%)

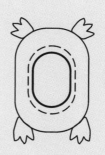

Teddy Bear (page 88)
(Enlarge 200%)

Prone Unicorn (page 90)
(Enlarge 200%)

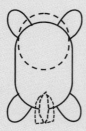

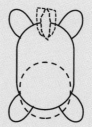
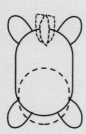

Upright Unicorn Body (page 90)
(Enlarge 200%)

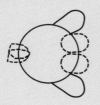

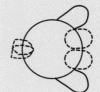
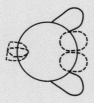

Upright Unicorn Head (page 90)
(Enlarge 200%)

Shiba Inu (page 92)
(Enlarge 200%)

Penguin Body (page 94)
(Enlarge 200%)

Penguin Flippers (page 94)
(Enlarge 200%)

Gingerbread Man (page 98)
(Enlarge 200%)

Duckling (page 100)
(Enlarge 200%)

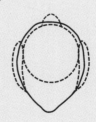 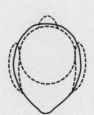

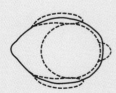 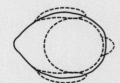

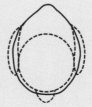 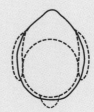

Polar Bear (page 110)
(Enlarge 200%)

Koala (page 114)
(Enlarge 200%)

  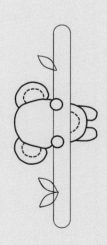 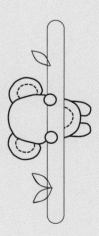

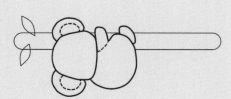 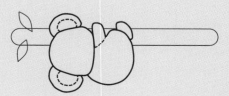

Leaf (page 114)
(Enlarge 200%)

Sloth (page 118)
(Enlarge 200%)

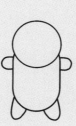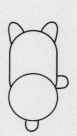

Octopus (page 128)
(Enlarge 200%)

Weights & Measures

Quantities for this book are given in metric and American (spoon) measures. Standard spoon measurements used are: 1 teaspoon = 5 ml and 1 tablespoon = 15 ml. All measures are level unless otherwise stated.

LIQUID AND VOLUME MEASURES

Metric	Imperial	American
5 ml	$^1/_6$ fl oz	1 teaspoon
10 ml	$^1/_3$ fl oz	1 dessertspoon
15 ml	$^1/_2$ fl oz	1 tablespoon
60 ml	2 fl oz	$^1/_4$ cup (4 tablespoons)
85 ml	$2^1/_2$ fl oz	$^1/_3$ cup
90 ml	3 fl oz	$^3/_8$ cup (6 tablespoons)
125 ml	4 fl oz	$^1/_2$ cup
180 ml	6 fl oz	$^3/_4$ cup
250 ml	8 fl oz	1 cup
300 ml	10 fl oz ($^1/_2$ pint)	$1^1/_4$ cups
375 ml	12 fl oz	$1^1/_2$ cups
435 ml	14 fl oz	$1^3/_4$ cups
500 ml	16 fl oz	2 cups
625 ml	20 fl oz (1 pint)	$2^1/_2$ cups
750 ml	24 fl oz ($1^1/_5$ pints)	3 cups
1 litre	32 fl oz ($1^3/_5$ pints)	4 cups
1.25 litres	40 fl oz (2 pints)	5 cups
1.5 litres	48 fl oz ($2^2/_5$ pints)	6 cups
2.5 litres	80 fl oz (4 pints)	10 cups

DRY MEASURES

Metric	Imperial
30 grams	1 ounce
45 grams	$1^1/_2$ ounces
55 grams	2 ounces
70 grams	$2^1/_2$ ounces
85 grams	3 ounces
100 grams	$3^1/_2$ ounces
110 grams	4 ounces
125 grams	$4^1/_2$ ounces
140 grams	5 ounces
280 grams	10 ounces
450 grams	16 ounces (1 pound)
500 grams	1 pound, $1^1/_2$ ounces
700 grams	$1^1/_2$ pounds
800 grams	$1^3/_4$ pounds
1 kilogram	2 pounds, 3 ounces
1.5 kilograms	3 pounds, $4^1/_2$ ounces
2 kilograms	4 pounds, 6 ounces

OVEN TEMPERATURE

	°C	°F	Gas Regulo
Very slow	120	250	1
Slow	150	300	2
Moderately slow	160	325	3
Moderate	180	350	4
Moderately hot	190/200	370/400	5/6
Hot	210/220	410/440	6/7
Very hot	230	450	8
Super hot	250/290	475/550	9/10

LENGTH

Metric	Imperial
0.5 cm	$^1/_4$ inch
1 cm	$^1/_2$ inch
1.5 cm	$^3/_4$ inch
2.5 cm	1 inch

ABBREVIATION

tsp	teaspoon
Tbsp	tablespoon
g	gram
kg	kilogram
ml	millilitre